drawings

Thames & Hudson

contents

manolo blahník

6   foreword *anna wintour*

8   about manolo *andré leon talley*

12   manolo at work *michael roberts*

18   without tradition we are nothing
anna piaggi

22   the drawings

24   the 70s

52   the 80s

80   the 90s

128   the 2000s

184   liking 'feets' *eric boman*

188   the step into possibility
amanda, lady harlech

192   captions

196   special thanks

foreword

I can't pinpoint the moment when Manolo Blahník became a member of my extended fashion family, perhaps because he is a wonderfully ageless man who has never seemed young or old. But I do recall my children crawling around his Old Church Street studio when, as editor of British *Vogue* in the Eighties, I would drop by for a cup of tea. Manolo's atelier was, and has remained, a place of almost magical enchantment; and my secret suspicion that he is related to Geppetto and other artisans of myth is fortified by his otherworldly manners. Nobody embodies the virtues of old-world charm and humility as unfailingly as Manolo. Of course, nobody would be more entitled to indulge in the vices of self-satisfaction and pride. Manolo Blahník is quite simply one of the greatest shoe designers of all time. I need hardly note that the word 'Manolos' has entered the language as a synonym for fabulous footwear. This achievement rests on his relentless engagement with both a personal aesthetic and the butterfly flutterings of fashion. He could never make a chunky platform just because the runways were trembling under the weight of clodhopper models; but nor would he deny his fans the frisson that comes with wearing a shoe that is perfectly of-the-moment. His generosity extends to the younger generation of designers: from Galliano in the Nineties to the likes of Zac Posen today, his shoes have literally elevated their catwalk creations. He is the Brooke Astor of the fashion world and, in my view, deserves a knighthood. Who better to be told to 'arise' than the master of the heel? In the meantime, it's we – his lucky clients – who get to be ennobled by his genius. The truth is, I wear no other shoes except his; and I see from my daughter's incursions into my cupboard that the former crawler has found her feet, which is to say her Manolos.

ANNA WINTOUR
Editor in Chief, American *Vogue*

about manolo

Cristobal Balenciaga and Manolo Blahník...two legendary Spaniards – one the greatest couturier of the twentieth century, the other the most influential shoe designer of his time. I've known many women in New York who have confessed that wearing Blahník's designs is, very often, better than sex. Not just the thought of it, but the very act! Manolo creates visual poems for women's feet. Some women desire fabulous jewels; others think of his shoes as jewels for the feet. With his world of fantasy, rich detail and extraordinary imagination, he destroyed the whole idea that diamonds are a girl's best friend. Manolo Blahník's shoes are. Every woman must feel like a movie star, with her feet hitting the seamless red carpet when she slips into a pair of his wondrously sexy, elegant creations. Manolo Blahník is just plain good, old-fashioned, rip-roaring fun. His phrasing, his pace in language is like the rippling staccato, the fast sound you associate with a computer keyboard. He thinks and speaks in speed dial. His homes are some of the most extraordinary places. In Bath as well as in London, Manolo's decorations are the kind that have become legend. I have also spent some of the most fun, the happiest days as a guest at his home on one of Bath's most elegant crescents. He is a great host. Every detail is perfection. Presentation is everything. He believes in simple food, and nothing is as much fun as watching Manolo stir up one of his favourite fruit cakes. Then dashing upstairs to build a roaring fire in the drawing room, where one can sit back and talk for hours, watch one movie after another into early morning hours, wake up the next day and take long healthy walks around Bath. He is more than a great friend. When he was in a London hospital, for a vertebrae problem, I flew from New York for a week to sit there, every afternoon, reading him Camille Paglia's writings. Two or three hours reading to him was like going to a private version of *Absolutely Fabulous*, long before it was a big television hit. He is his own one man Ab Fab. Diana Vreeland and Manolo Blahník will always be to me like a personal family. She was my surrogate mother; he, the wonderful brother I never had. I'll never forget when I told him that nothing would please Diana Vreeland more than Stilton cheese, he arrived in New York with the best Stilton cheese packed in ice, which he promptly delivered to Vreeland's legendary apartment with a small case of wonder 'glides', as Vreeland called the famous mule he created for her friend Pauline de Rothschild. Three shoes are my favourite Blahníks. First, the pearl-encrusted mule he originally designed for Pauline de Rothschild when she first went into Manolo Blahník's London shop. Three decades later that shoe remains as modern as it was for this great American original, a former dress designer from Baltimore, who became a style icon not only in couture, but in everything she touched, including her own homes. Second, there is the shoe he designed for John Galliano, a mule stripped to the bare essence of its construction. Mounted on a metal nail stiletto heel, the entire foot is held by one transparent vinyl strap, and one transparent thong on the big toe: a virtuoso modern Blahník. And third, he recently created his own version of a winter, high-stepping hip hop, stiletto ankle boot. It takes its inspiration from the industrial mountain boot, worn by so many young people around the world today. With Manolo, the boot gets its strong sexual energy from the wood-mounted heel, the padded collar of the boot and the white top stitching. Manolo Blahník creates beauty. Some of his shoes are simple, elegant; others are fantastic, the beyond. His work has a unique aesthetic. In his world of shoes, there is one constant. He captures the most powerful of emotions: desire.

ANDRÉ LEON TALLEY
Editor at Large, American *Vogue*

11

manolo at work

Manolo Blahník flies to Milan ten times a year and every morning, for up to four weeks at a stretch, takes a fast car to the suburbs, where he ricochets between several regional outposts manufacturing his Spring and Fall collections. At the oldest of these traditional *fabbriche* his desk is layered with sketches, swatches of fabric, plastic prototypes and wooden shoe lasts. He wraps plain paper round a last, sticks it down with tape, and in pencil, designs straight onto the shape of the foot. At this point he is more artisan than artist. Moving downstairs he dons a white coat, secures the rough wooden carving of a heel in a metal vice and scours it down with an iron file to create the quintessentially fine Manoloesque shape. At this stage he is more sculptor than shoemaker. Returning once again to his workroom, he burrows through giddy mounds of Blahníkian materials – horn and hyena, raffia, silk, linen, bronze tassels, white crystal beads, tiny oriental bells. Agitated, he shreds an offending piece of chintz. 'Horrendous,' he shudders. 'And what is that for?' I ask, holding up a tassel. 'That is for THIS,' he says, hurling it savagely across the room. At such times he is both whirling dervish and world famous designer.

I clearly remember Manolo showing me his first shoe designs 30 years ago. Temporarily employed in an achingly trendy Kensington boutique, he cut an exotic figure on the fashion scene with his wild woolly hair, excitable personality and tight dandy clothes. Often as animated as in a silent movie – albeit without much use for the word 'silent' – on that day he was unusually subdued, reaching into a folder for a sheaf of sketches and bashfully murmuring about 'doing shoes as a sideline'. The designs were odd. Chunky but whimsical, modern yet botanical, all at the same time. He indicated the soles and heels would be in crepe, the uppers in cartoonish suedes. The shoes looked charming but utterly impractical. However, they had such ingenuity and dash you hoped they would work. Then, within moments, it seemed every celebrated foot trailed his bright suede leaves and tottered around on heels which bent through lack of technical support. Manolo has always admitted it took him ten years to really know how to make a pair of shoes. Yet from the outset he was never short of ideas: Pop Art, Op Art, Geisha clogs, Barbarella boots, Kenyan sandals, Hapsburg mules – creativity gushes out at such a rate even today when designing a collection of 150 styles there are usually 100 extras that he must 'kill'. 'And what's this called?' I ask, indicating one of a pile of slippers with names like *Anthurium* and *Philadendrum*. 'It's called, it's called…*Afterthought*,' he says, glumly uninspired for a nanosecond. Whenever the muse deserts him, Manolo is apt to say things like 'I am simply levitating with rage' and glare at the stack of leather soles, thin as communion wafers, perched near his elbow. His collection for Summer 2003 will be something to do with Guadeloupe, the 18th century, Malmaison and the jungle temperament of the Empress Josephine. He is also majoring in bells, or more precisely 'the leg with bells because those girls in Guadeloupe get lost'. For a while he was thinking of large cowbells, voodoo and chicken bones but that soon passed, being far too weighty for the soaring clouds of his imagination. 'He is the Picasso of shoes,' Grace Coddington once told me in Paris. Perhaps. But that succulent colouration, those rich embellishments imply the soles might be Picasso, yet his soul is more Matisse.

Picture Manolo, endlessly motoring to work past the brute concrete of Milanese council flats decorated with graffiti, past the Cimitero Monumentale which once housed the body of Eva Peron. Picture him hunched daily over his desk, immersed in his world of impeccable insteps and latticed straps aided by the faithful Ambrogio, Giorgio and Agostino. Then you can understand when he says: 'The only thing I totally adore about my work is the process of doing it.'

MICHAEL ROBERTS
Fashion Editor, *The New Yorker*

15

without tradition

we are nothing

Luchino Visconti to
Manolo Blahník, 1971

Manolo Blahník met Luchino Visconti at The Roundhouse in Chalk Farm, London, in 1971 – the year in which he designed his first cherry and leaf embellished sandals for Ossie Clarke. 'Why are most of your films in costume?' Blahník asked the director. 'Because without tradition, we are nothing,' was his reply.

Blahník's passion for Visconti began in his native Canary Islands where, as a child, he first saw *Senso*, a film that opened for him the symbolic gates to Italy. It marked the beginning of a spiritual connection between Manolo and the peninsula, a love affair that is at once intense and passionate, yet full of delicate pleasures: aniseed sweets from Milan, Sicilian carnations (or their distillate from Santa Maria Novella, in Florence).

Slices of life, experienced in a kind of Italian or Viscontian trance: the large vase full of tuberoses in the 'Il Lavoro' episode of *Boccaccio '70*...the homage to Volterra in *Vaghe Stelle dell'Orsa*, the Sicily of *Il Gattopardo* and the Milan of *Rocco*. Global tastes, colours...

For Manolo, even the textures, the materials used to create the shoes – all made in Italy – become a sensory experience. For him, 'Italy is the most sensuous country in the world.'

ANNA PIAGGI
Creative Consultant, Italian *Vogue*

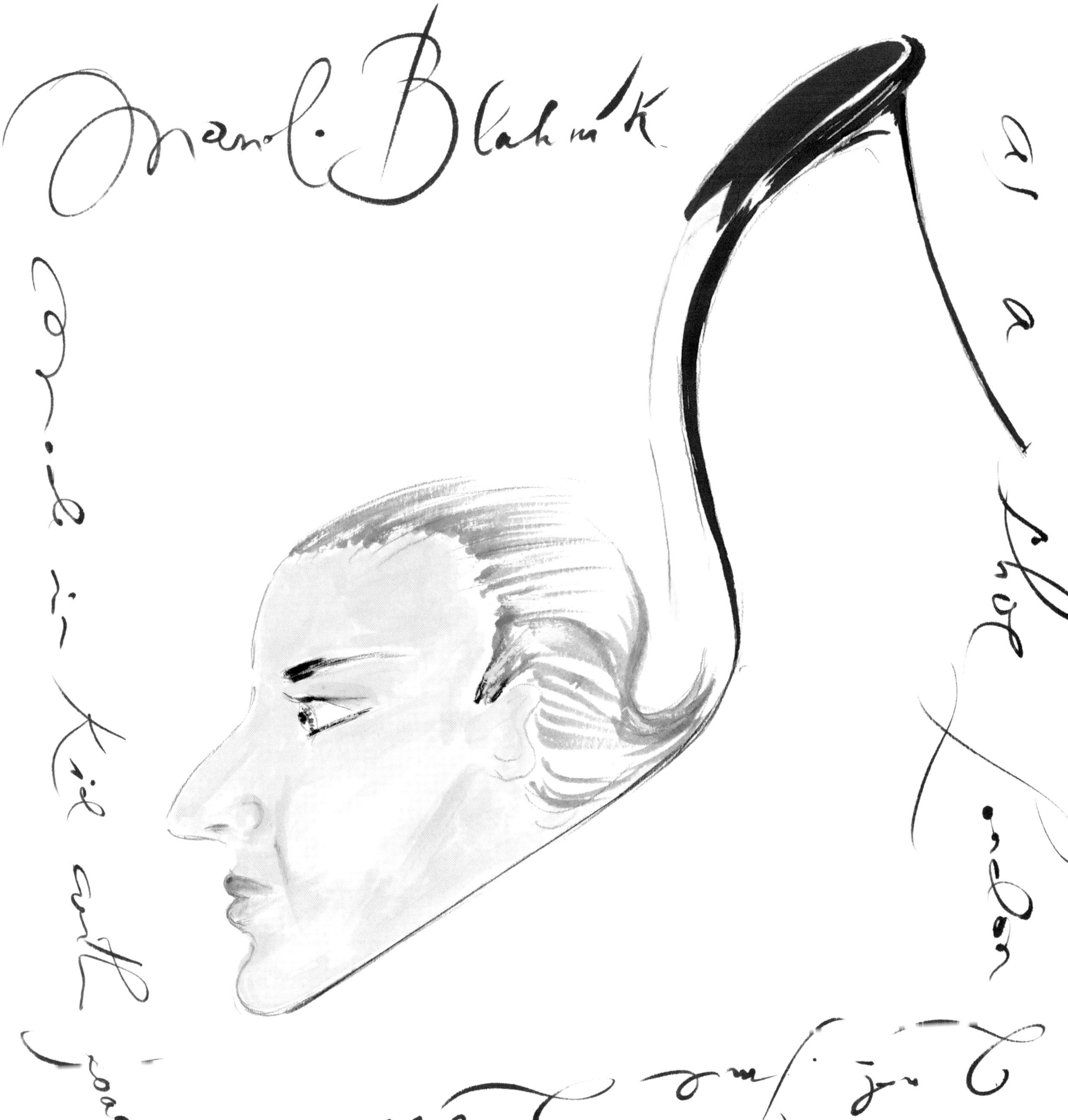
Manolo Blahnik

the drawings

Manolo Blahník *noun*: artist, inventor, artisan. Shoes-boots-mules-sandals-magic-maker. *adjective*: creative, artistic, extravagant, classy, elegant, genial, unique, eccentric, chic, styled, glamorous.

FRANCA SOZZANI

the

70s

London 1971 . Pellon crépe 6 inches . Two tone

fa Ossie Clarke . Rosal

suede, leather in contrasting

Rubber covered heels-

about shoe -

28

'Manolo speaks through his shoes. For him, the foot, the shoe, implies the whole nature of a person, and expresses a story.' ANNA PIAGGI

The *bride that is in cork* caress worth

P

Manolo Blahnik ©

tent leather fr the

evalin p Konai Jinanor(bodon)"

London 1971 —

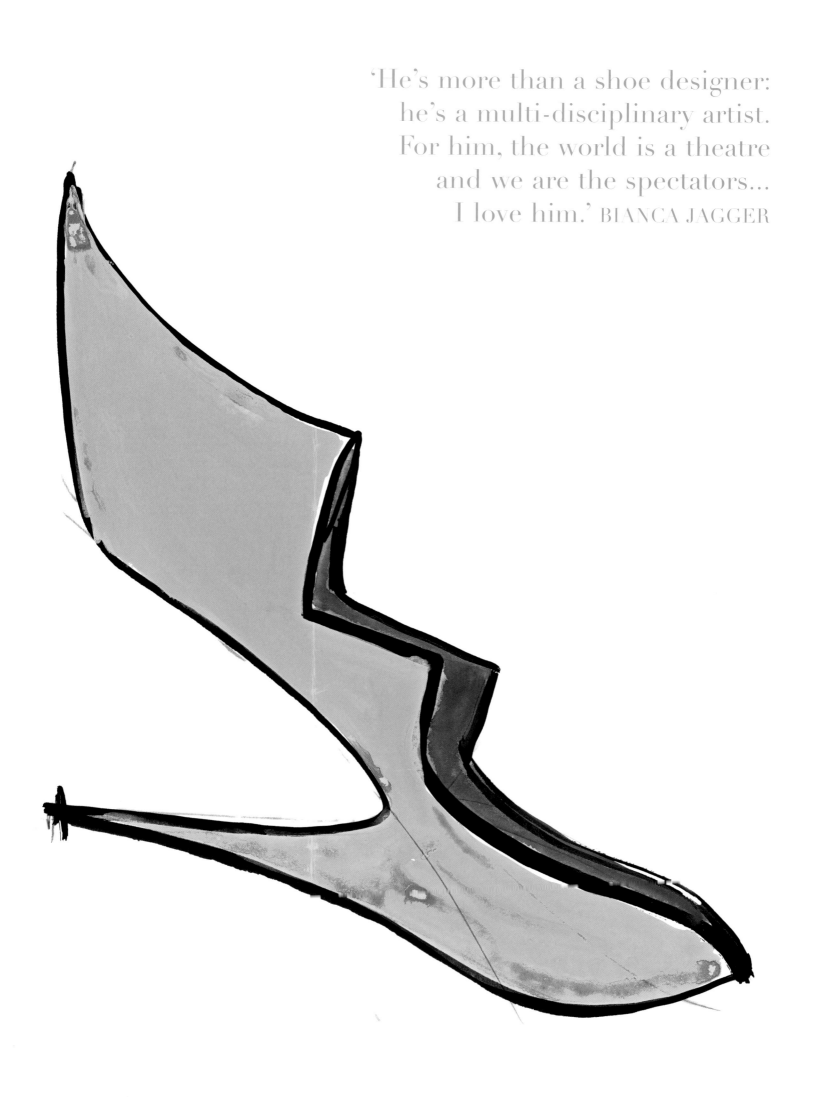

'He's more than a shoe designer: he's a multi-disciplinary artist. For him, the world is a theatre and we are the spectators... I love him.' BIANCA JAGGER

34

'Manolo not only fulfils our own dreams of what shoes should be, but he weaves still more dreams for us with shoes we could never have imagined. His drawings exude elegance, style and wit, and these he translates into shoes which are beautiful, exquisitely made.'
ANNA HARVEY

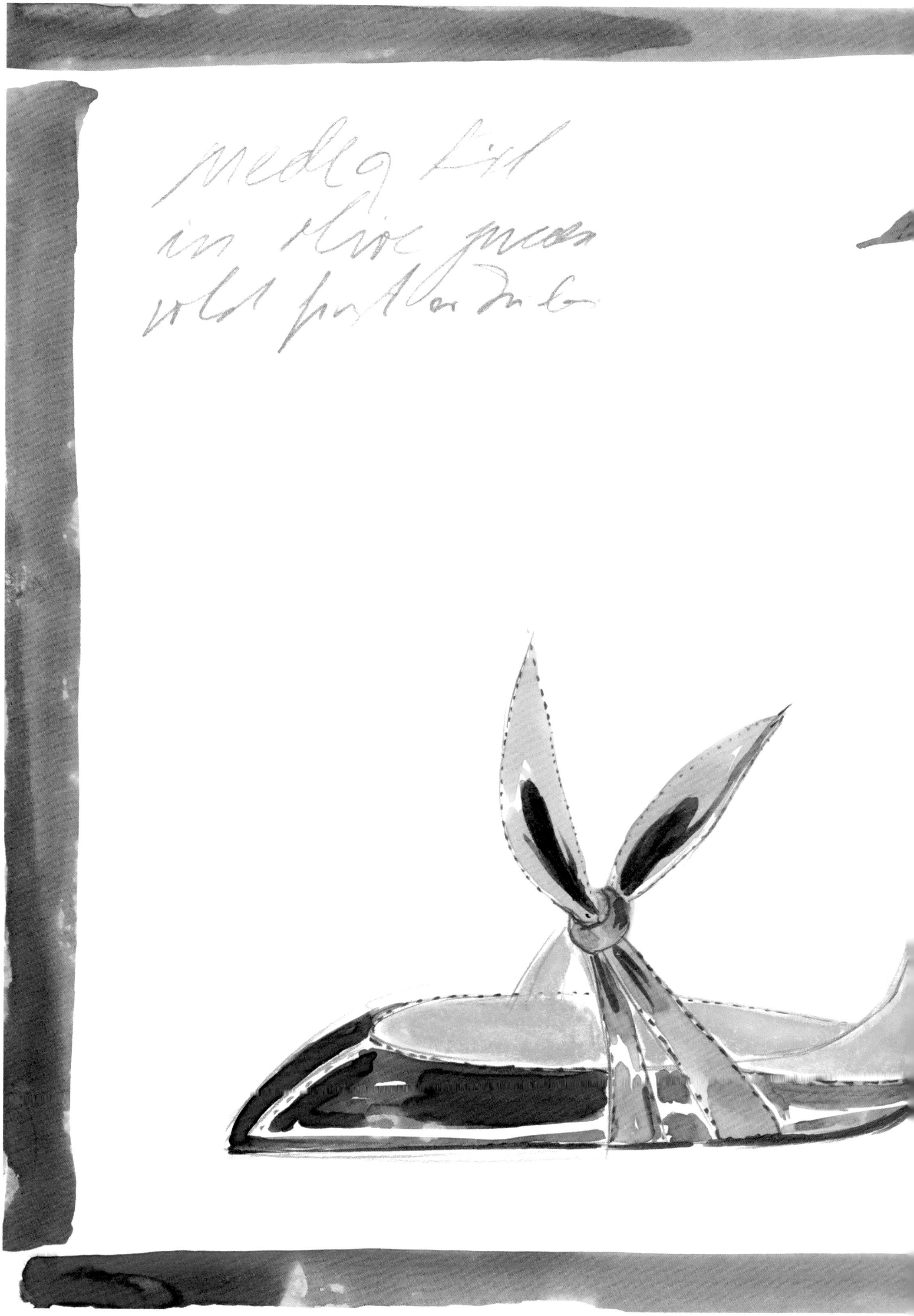

Manolo Blahnik 15-

Cherry shoe madein 3 coulons suede

Ossie Black for Ossie Clarke
London 1971. Royal court shoe.

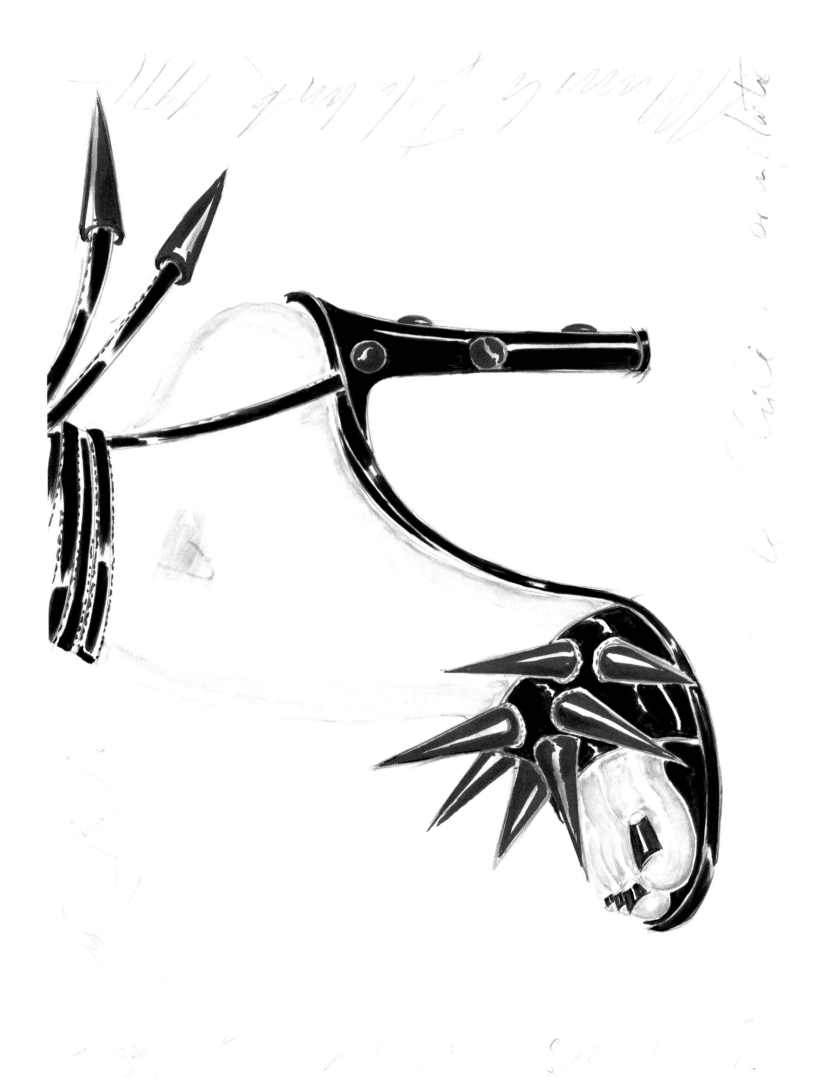

'I love the wildness of his shoes, the exotic colours and savage prints. He is the urban king of the jungle.'
NINIVAH KHOMO

Winter 1974

Manolo Blahnik 1974

'The sole of perfection.'
BEATRIX MILLER

'Other shoemakers don't have
the imagination, or the incredible
detail – such tiny weeny buckles,
they're all perfect.' LUCY FERRY

'E' un Genio!
We love him!
E' il più bravo stilista di
scarpe del MONDO!'
DOMENICO DOLCE &
STEFANO GABBANA

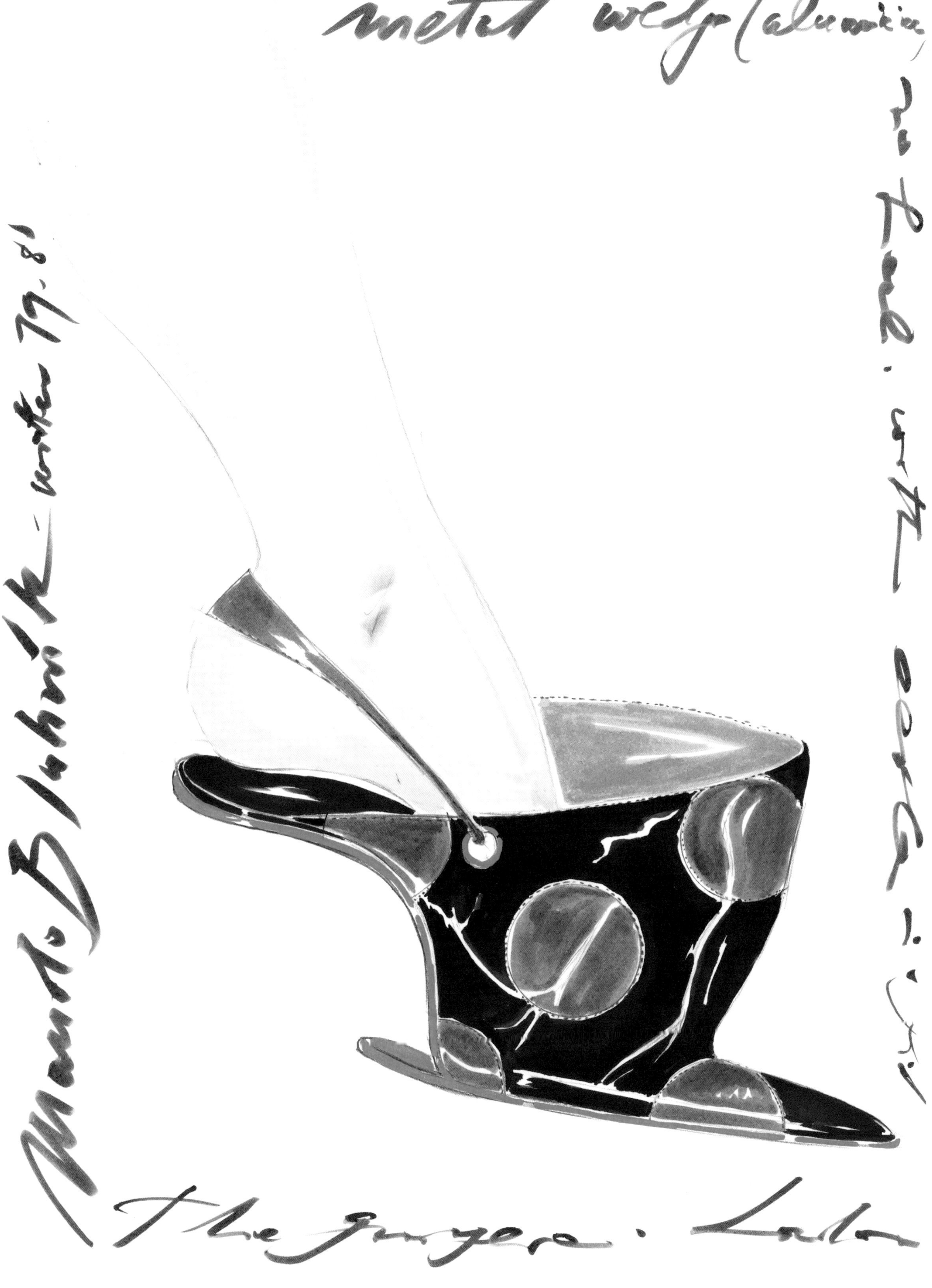

The stripes collection

Manolo Blahnik

Shoe-bag Brit

the Fabulous Britain '76

the

80s

'Only a few people in this business manage to stay always in fashion. When I once asked him how he managed it, he said: "It's like a wheel, things always come back. Fashion is about a reaction to what has just come before." I always wanted to be like him in what I do – getting it right on the nail.'
MARIO TESTINO

'He is the Picasso
of shoes.'
GRACE CODDINGTON

suede pumps and

red pompon in satin and silk pompon in wool

manolo Blahník 12. 1980

1985 — Monte Carlo

embroidered —
Satin High Heels.

The Demi mondaine.

ottoman . Black soft varnish lining

Tulle point d'esprit in dark grey

Manolo Blahnik 85

The Eye. B.T. in patent. Dark. Polish.

'You're like a horse that
has to be tamed, Manolo!'
DAVID BAILEY

Manolo Blahnik 1982 —
Tigerprinted calf with
linen ...

with semi-precious stones and baroque pearl and green pair

Maria Palmiori

Gold Hi-Heeled

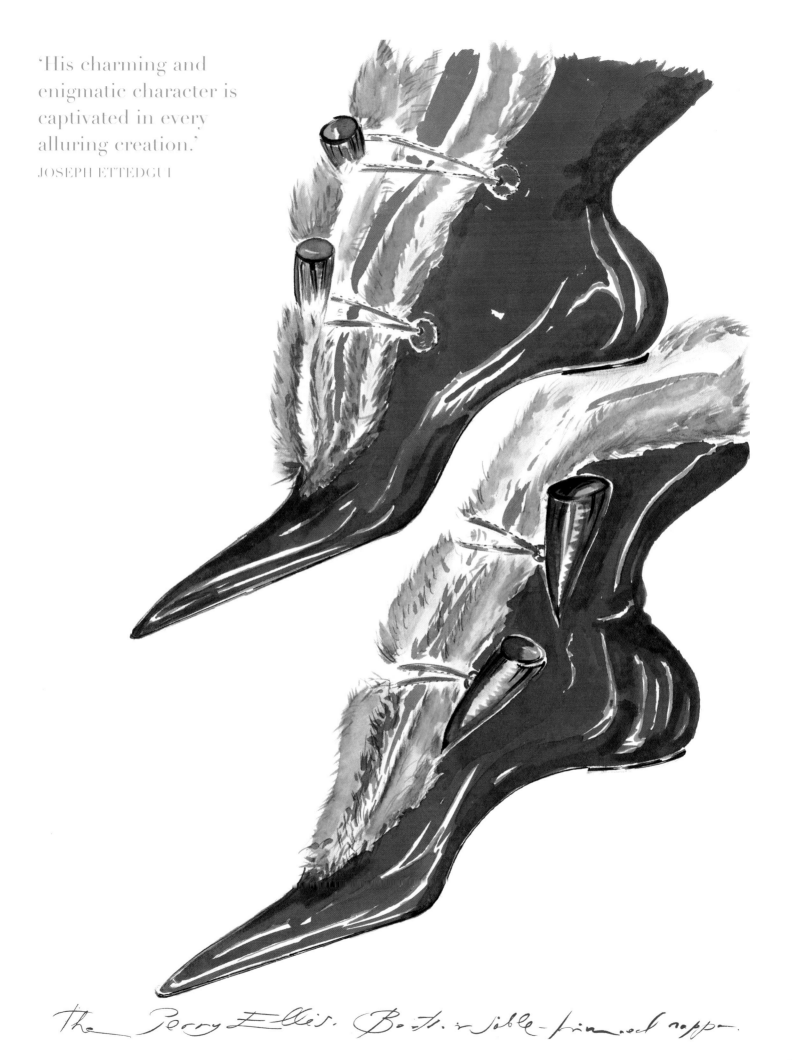

'I saw my first pair of Manolos in 1985 on Tina Chow's feet. From that moment on, a love affair began. 200 pairs later, I will always and forever be a Manolo girl.' VERONICA WEBB

'The thing you cannot duplicate is
the lightness of Manolos — take one in
your hand and lift it!' GEORGE MALKEMUS

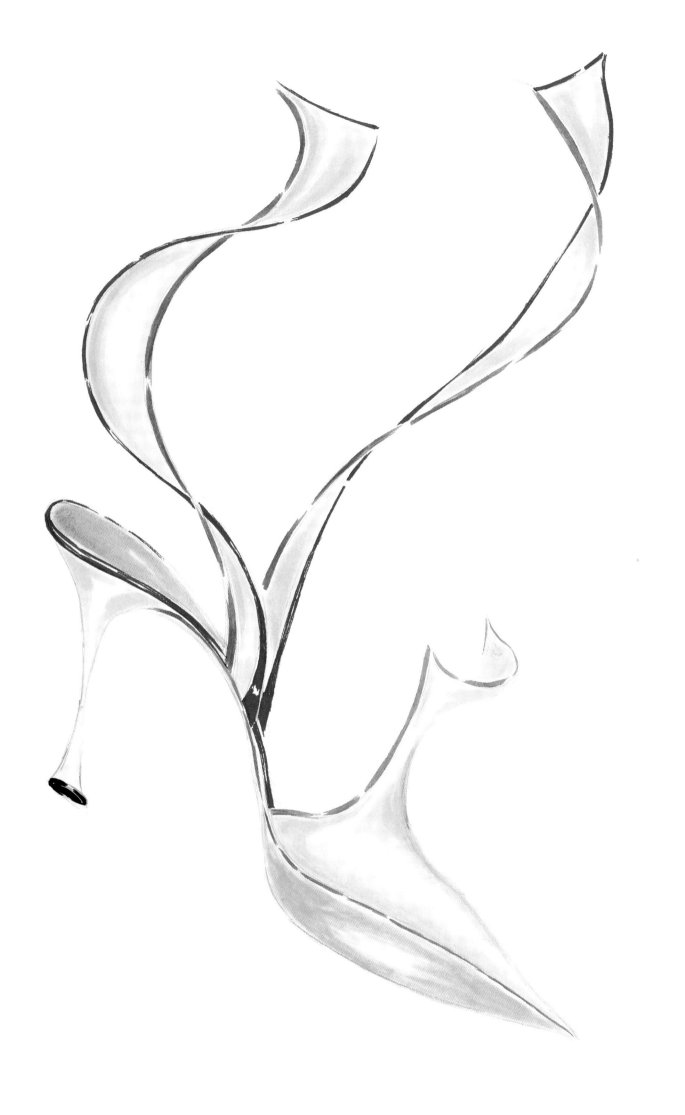

'With a perfect memory for everything he's seen or heard, his mind is an archive of facts and emotions. From the sensuality of Visconti to the purity of Sir Thomas Hope, from the romance of Canova to the wit and sophistication of Cecil Beaton, everything reappears in his art.' PETER SCHLESINGER

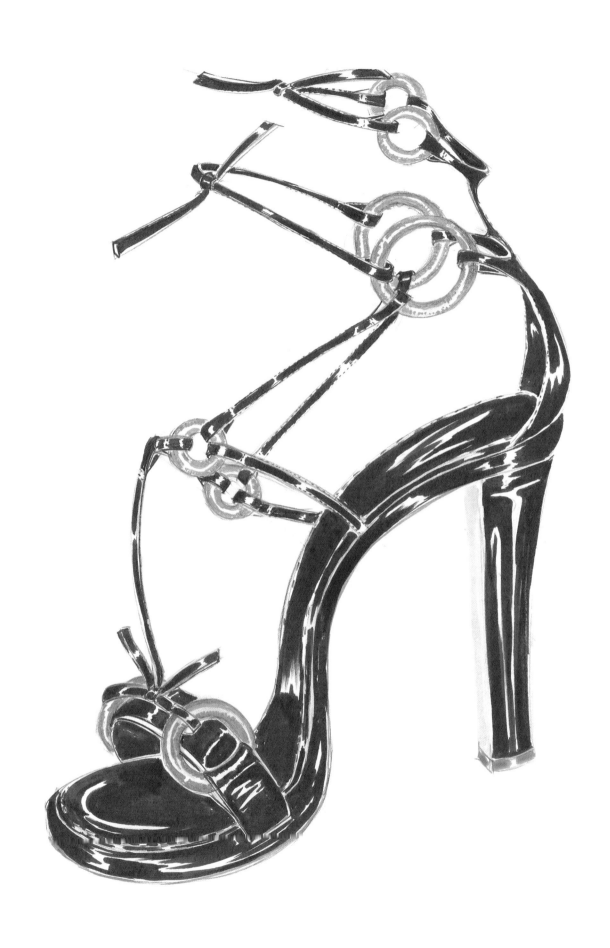

silk satin and velvet

Thank

Manolo

crêpe soled desert boot

'He's Benjamin Franklin, Isaac Newton – a genius. I fall at his feet and worship at his temple.' ISAAC MIZRAHI

'Manolo's shoes have such personality. They become individuals. He thinks of them like characters in a play or a movie.' LIZ TILBERIS

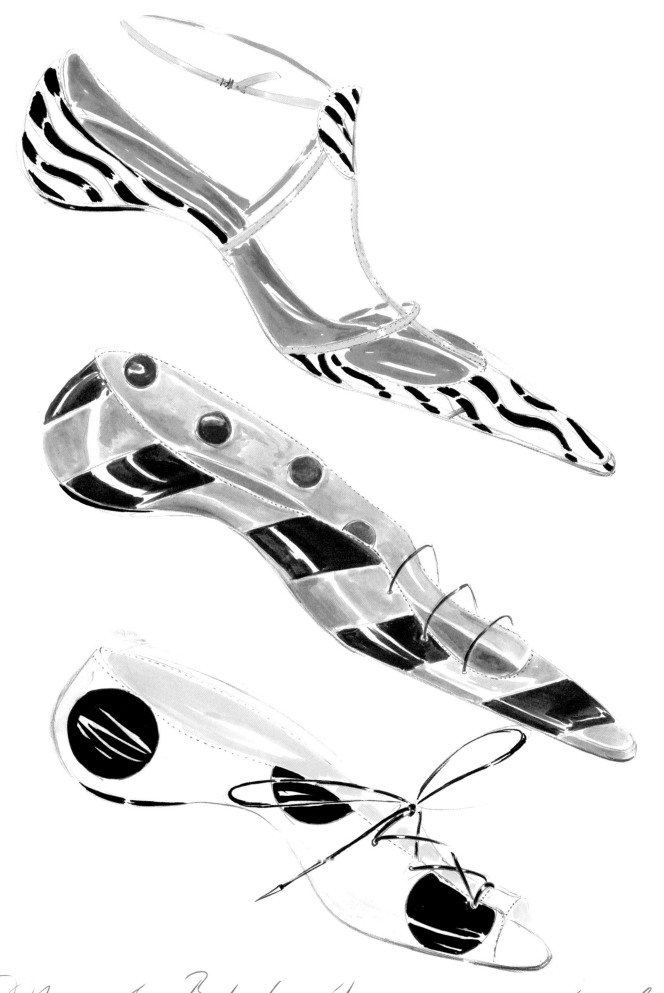

Manolo Blahnik 1985 London

'Hmmm, your glides
make me feel like
I'm walking on air.'
DIANA VREELAND

'Manolo is an inspiration.
Manolo is a great raconteur.
Manolo has exquisite taste.
Manolo is a hysterically
funny movie companion.
Manolo is family.' RIFAT OZBEK

Carl Blahnik 1986

Robert Clergerie Dancing collection

Taffeta & silk satin pump

the

90s

'How important is Manolo Blahník? I'll tell you.
If he wanted me to change the name of the store
to Neiman Blahník, I'd do it in a heartbeat.'
CYNTHIA MARCUS

'I wear Manolo – exclusively – for what I imagine are much the same reasons some women pile on serious jewelry and some men carry loaded guns. They endow the wearer with instant power, sex appeal, a distinct sense of possibility. When I put them on, I feel as though there's not a room in the world I can't glide through, not a single opponent – or man – I can't convince. Among my favourites are a pair of fabulous extravagant silver mesh mules trimmed in chinchilla. No shoes on earth make the feet look more beautiful – but, of course, one could say the same about them all. They make you feel like you do when you have on exquisite pieces of lingerie – except the whole world gets to see.'
JULIA REED

Style: "Arcadia" for Berluti. Dark grey & Blue ottoman raw silk faille

lady CMc. Laces in yellow silk. Nail heel

Donald Blaik. noirella: 98-TT.

83

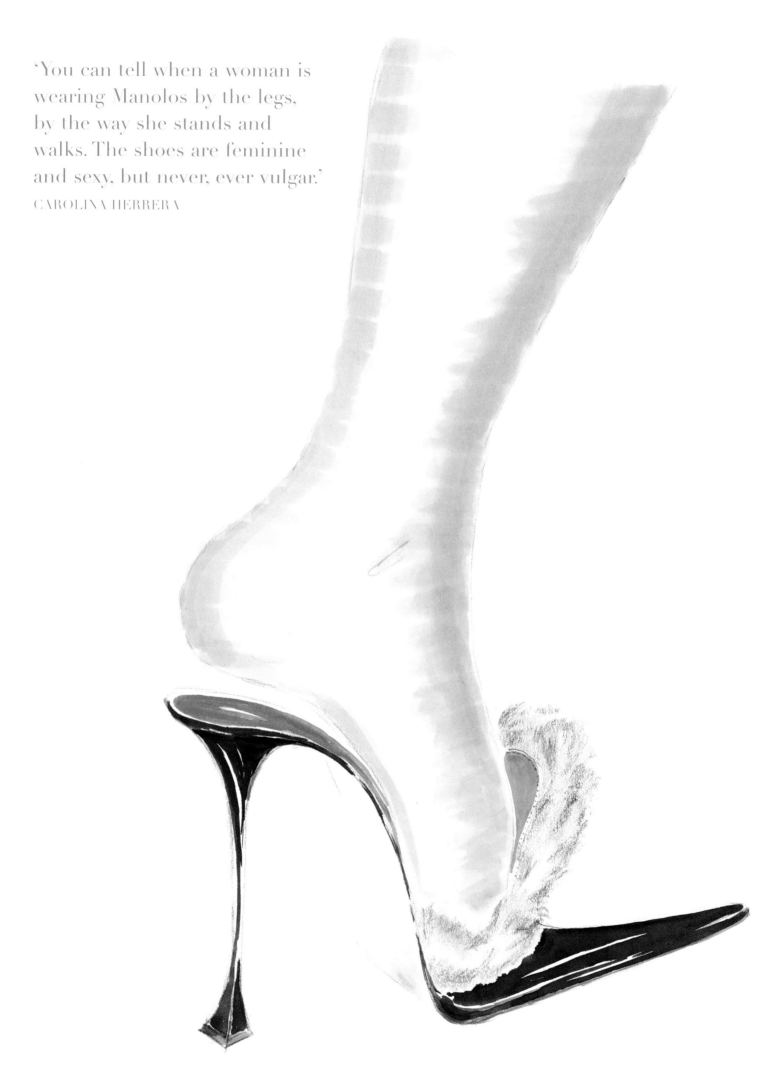

'You can tell when a woman is wearing Manolos by the legs, by the way she stands and walks. The shoes are feminine and sexy, but never, ever vulgar.'
CAROLINA HERRERA

Blahnik for John Galliano. The circus... ballet collection... Brando in lucite Brancusi heel

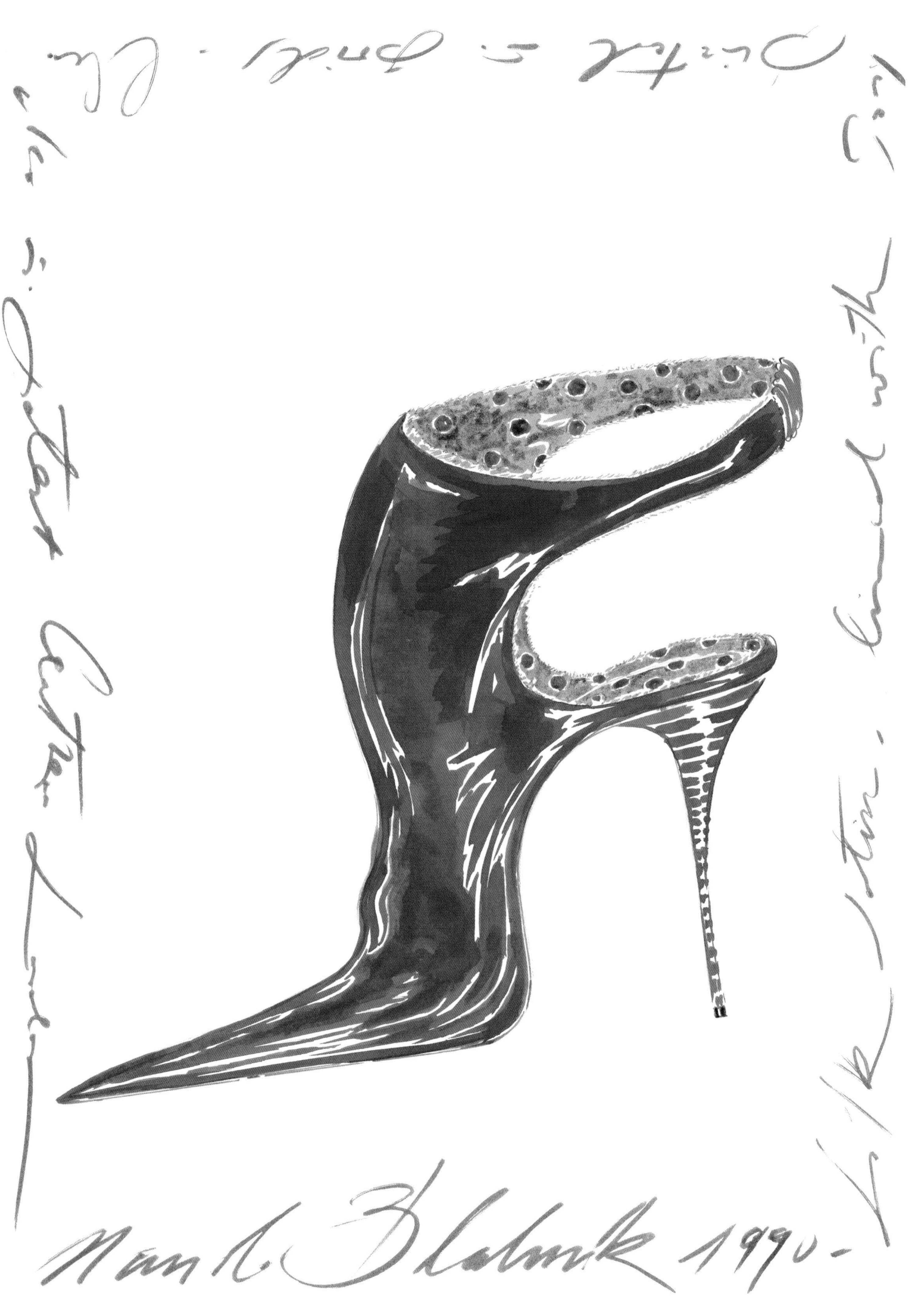

Manolo Blahnik 1990

London - 1997 - Sadie Frost + Linda Evangelista Chinese - The Hour of sure Satisfaction - "Shantou Lu" - courtesan!

'His shoes are as beautiful inside as out – something I learned from my shoe-repairer, who came out of his workroom to rave in admiration about a pair of boots he was resoling. "You never see work like this anymore," he said. Those boots, by the way, have lasted ten years without falling apart or going out of fashion.' SARAH MOWER

'Manolo's shoes are more than whimsical…
they are a rare combination of functionalism
and faultless aesthetics.' SARAJANE HOARE

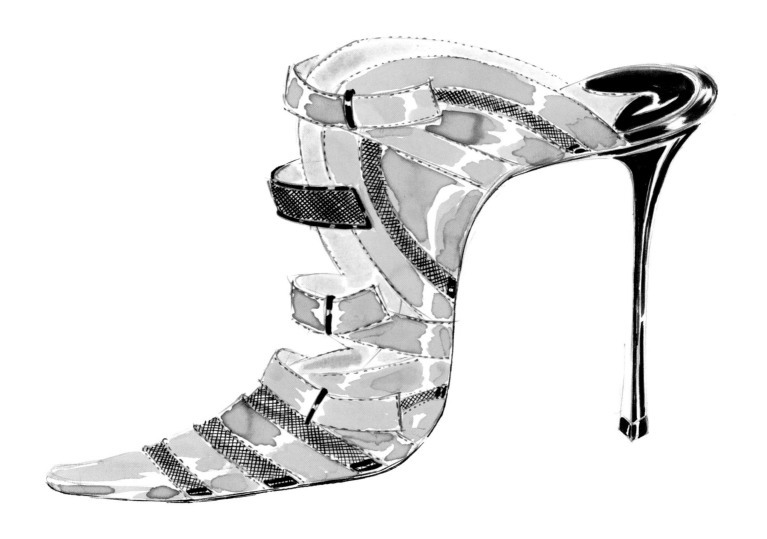

Soft ostrich skin with nylon and velcro

Manolo Blahnik London Milano '98

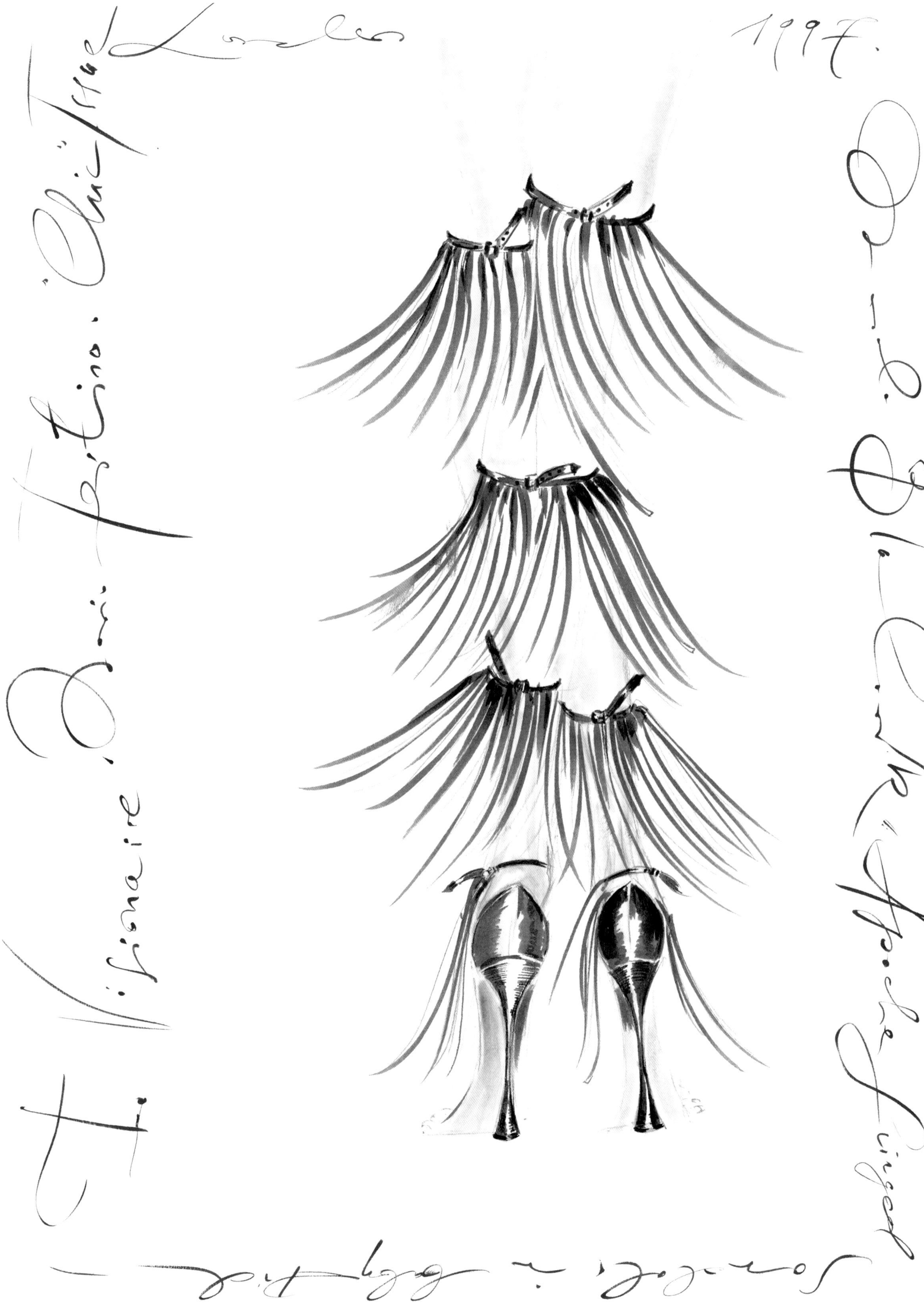
Visionaire
1997

'Incomparable Spain.

Painting during the Golden Age.
Renaissance religious sculpture.
Flamenco.
Manolo Blahník.'
CARLOS GARCIA-CALVO

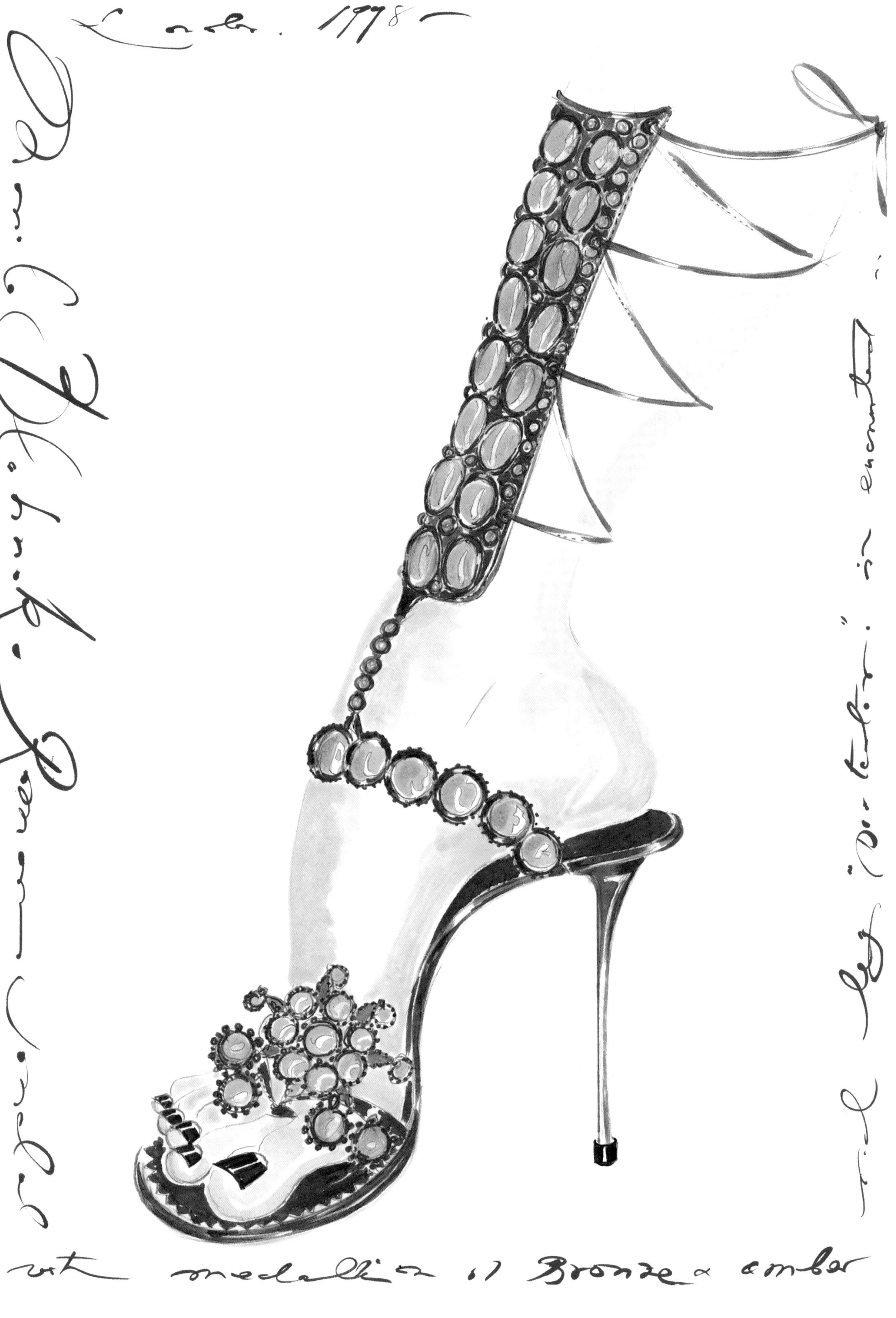
1998
medallion of Bronze & amber

Silk grosgrain and fragole in perline cristals and crochet

'Nature is perfect. Its engineering is a mystery — as it should remain. Manolo Blahník respects this. He has been given this touch and engineering genius by God. His work is as perfect and efficient as nature.'

ISABELLA BLOW · IMOGEN BUSH

Style "Senso" Winter 1978

'Manolo's shoes are unique. They are the sexiest things women wear, and at their best, they are works of art. His work is in a class by itself.'
JONATHAN NEWHOUSE

'I was lucky enough to work with him on my own label, as well as at Dior, for several seasons. Manolo always knew and understood how to anticipate what we were doing, even from the most abstract of phone calls. He is a true innovator. Working with him was like working with a kindred spirit who was so inspiring and such a creative force that he can light up a room with his presence.' JOHN GALLIANO

'Zipped up the back with no bones.
Sole love.' TILDA SWINTON

Project pour John Galliano "Dior Couture" 1997

Manolo Blahnik

→ Shoes for Summer 1997.

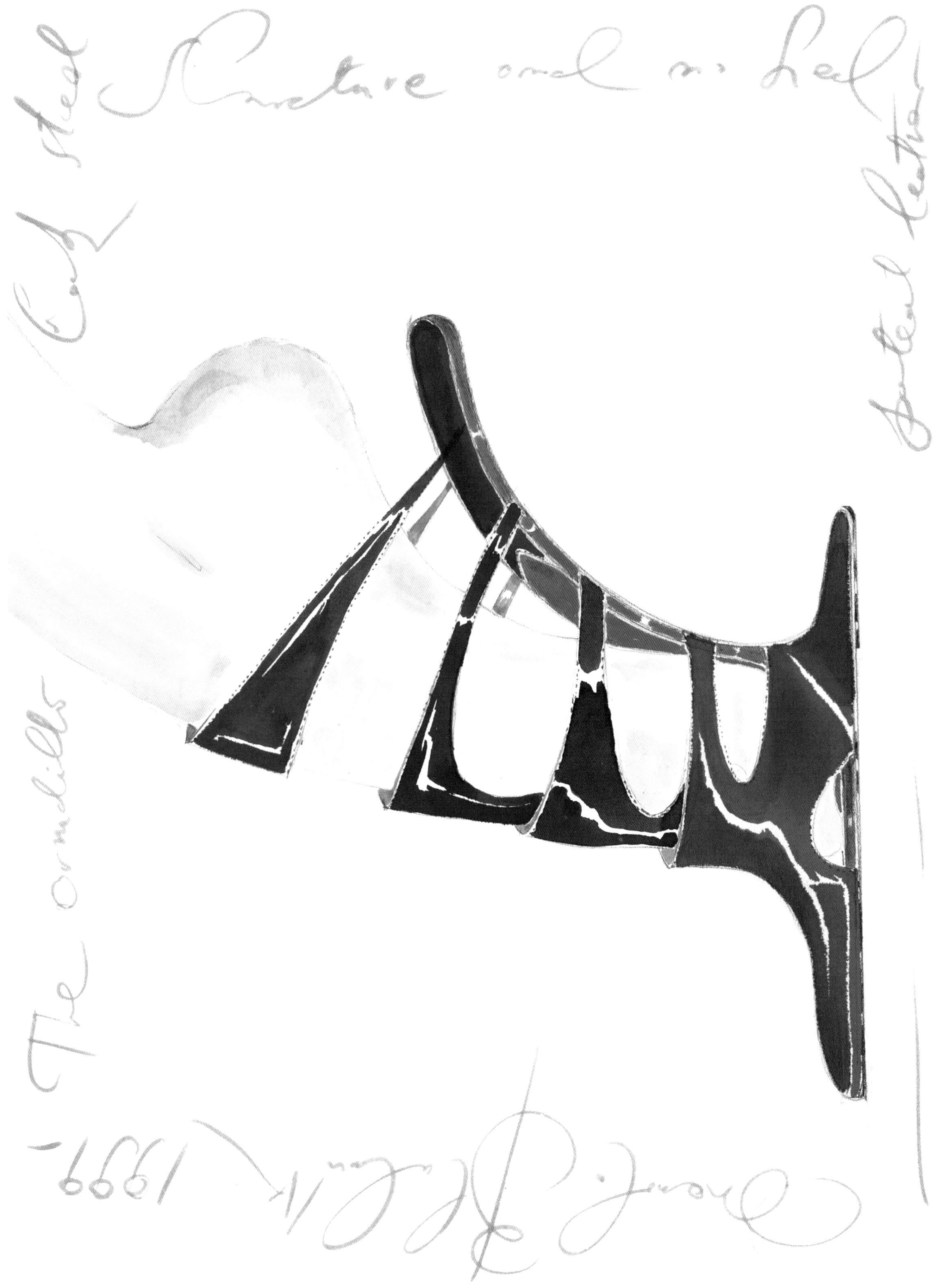

The armadillo
Structure and no heel
Patent leather
1999

Manolo Blahnik   1778

Perspex and metal heel

Londres
Paris

mule and gold kid

Manolo Blahnik

Summer. 1997. London.

Style: Tella. Two-tone. Sonya Kid.

Last. B.C. Heel Screw

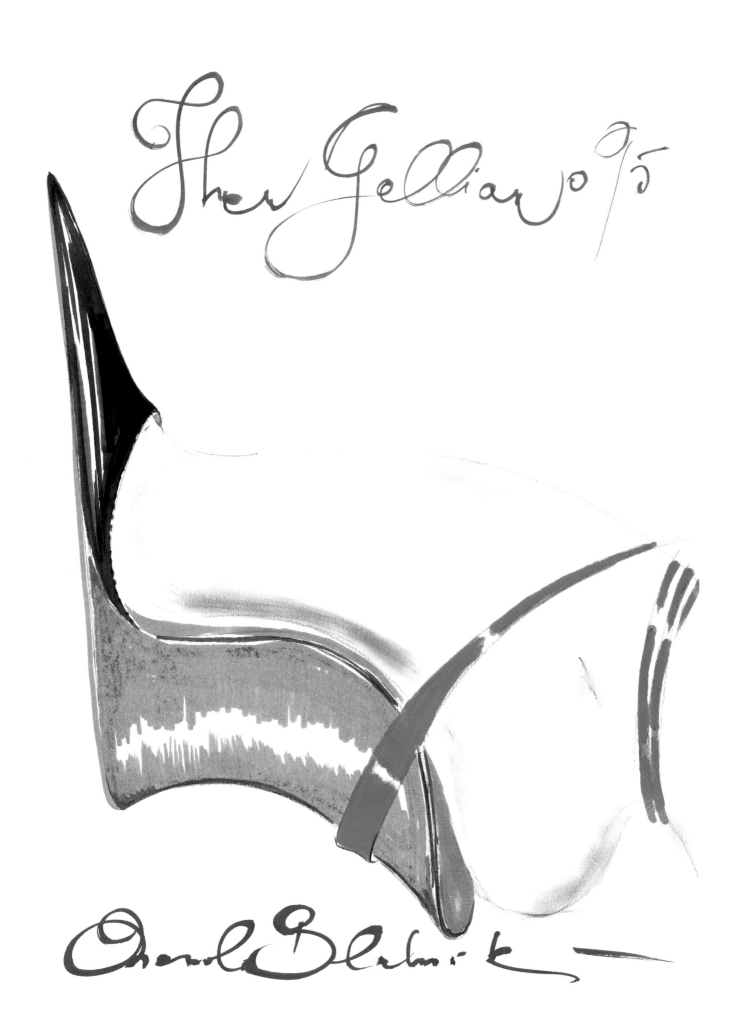

John Galliano 95

Manolo Blahnik

Manolo Blahnik 97

Amber & black wood (ebony). beads. 1997 for Dior

122

'Manolo Blahník's shoes are as good as sex…and they last longer.' MADONNA

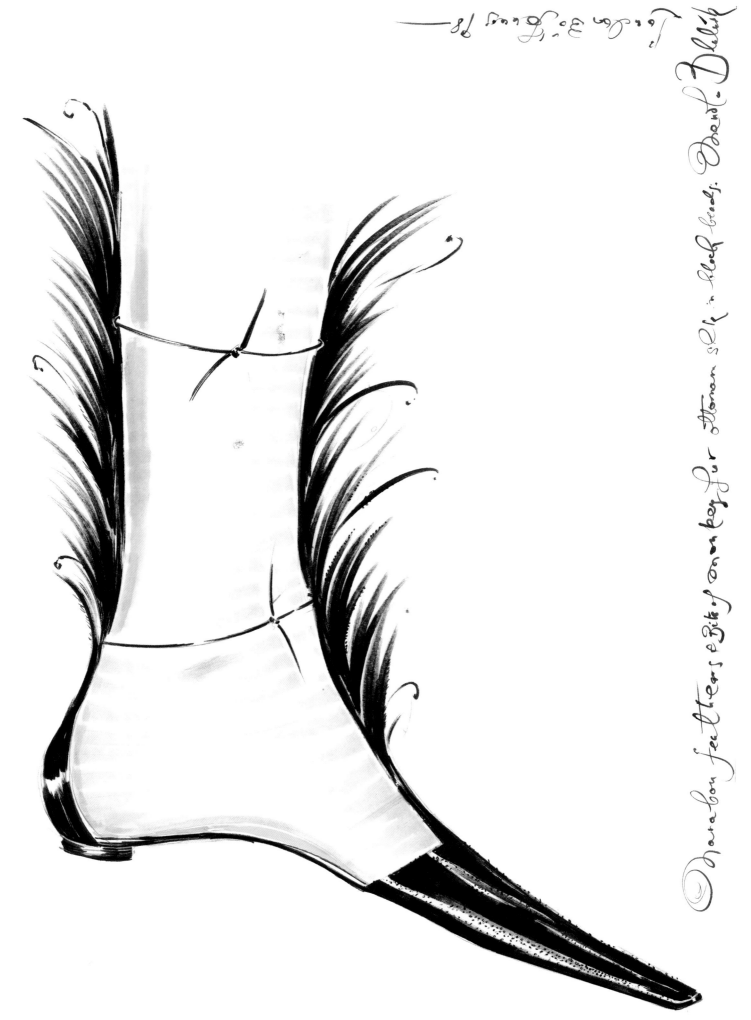

Marabou feathers & bits of monkey fur trim on silk in black beads. Dorothy Blake

London 30th June 78 —

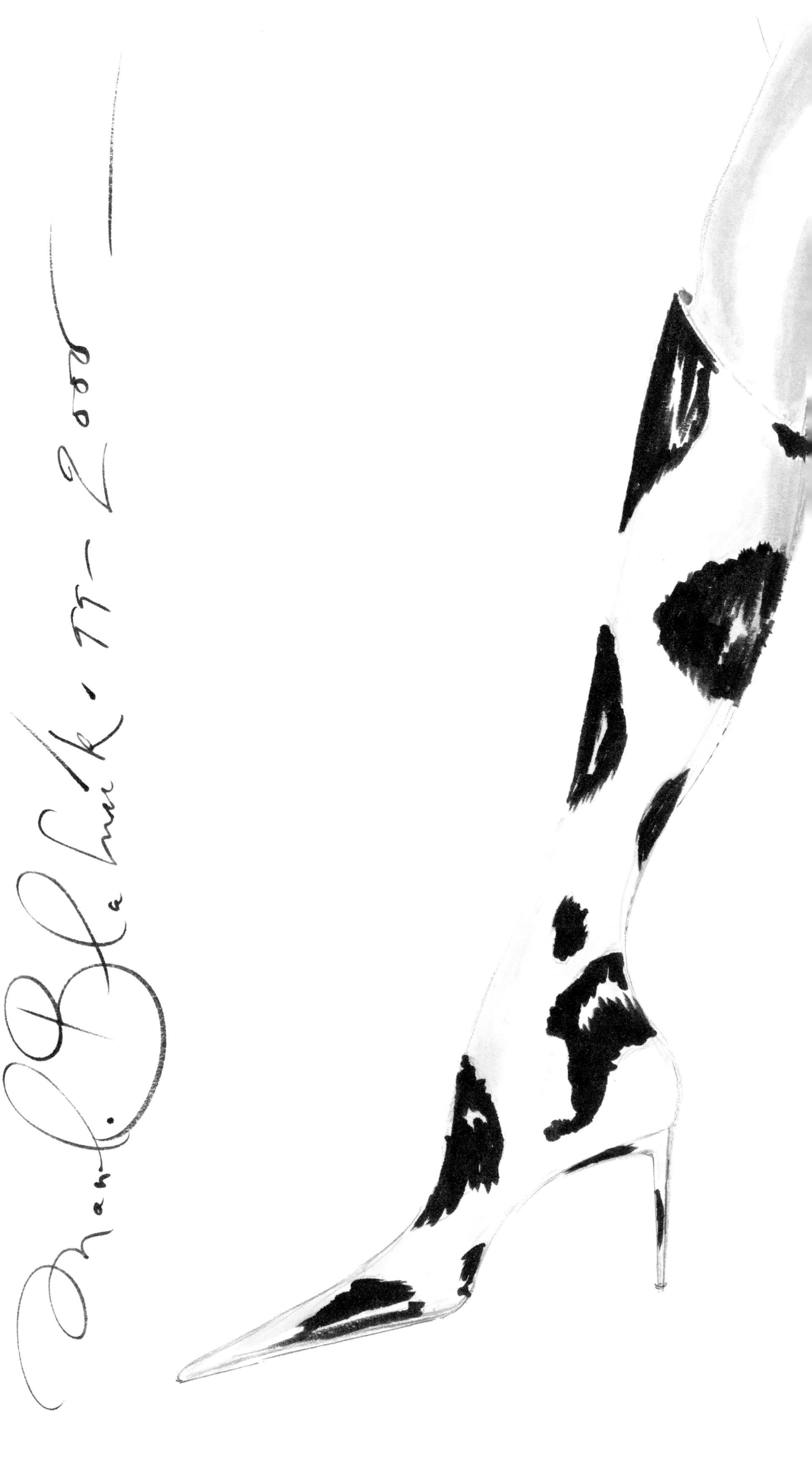

Jason's Boot – cowskin

'By now I can run a marathon in a pair of Manolo Blahník heels. I can race out and hail a cab. I can run up Sixth Avenue at full speed. I've destroyed my feet completely, but I don't really care. What do you need your feet for anyway?' SARAH JESSICA PARKER

the

2000s

'My shoes are not fashion,
they are gestures.'

Daniel Blaker 2001

Cutting edge - abstract shoe
made in silk ottoman 'crome yellow'
with scissors and 'blood' embroidery

131

'Q: What fashion
items would you
die without?

A: Diamond
earrings, jeans and
Manolo Blahníks.'

KATE MOSS

'Como Picasso y Almodovar,
Blahník pertenece al genio
Español mas universal.'
GUILLERMO CABRERA INFANTE

tonadillera
pare et flots 2001. 2002

michaf pogvor

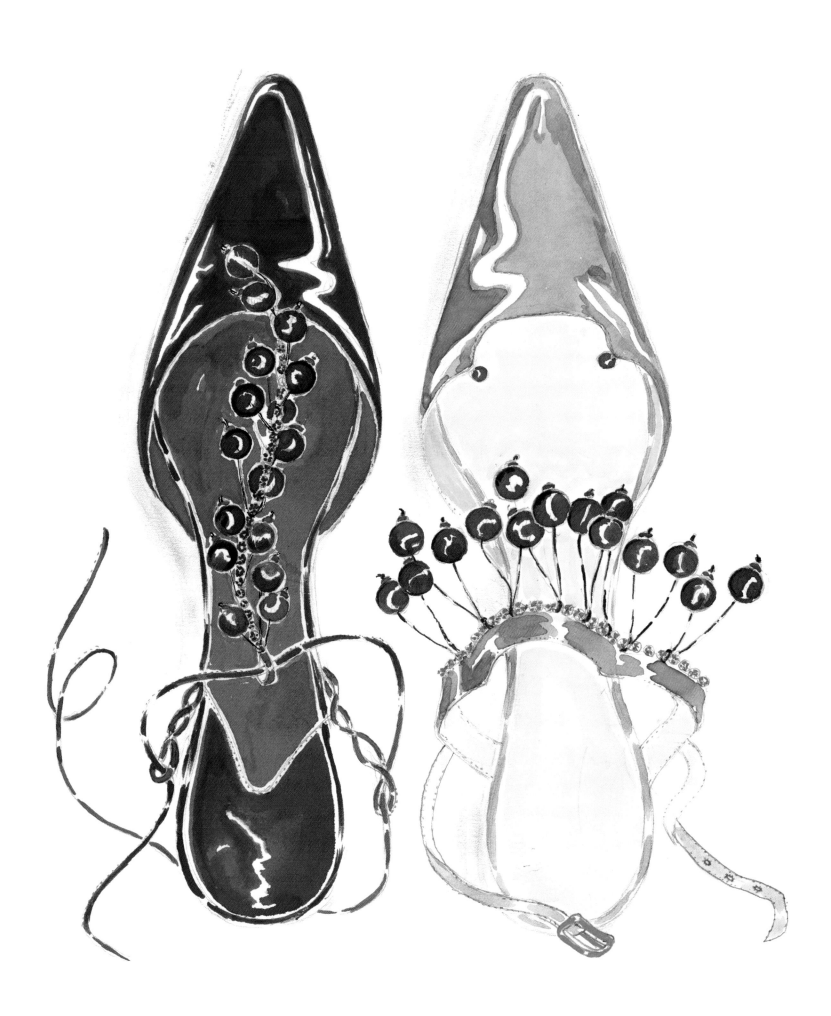

Croquis de ...

Donald Blahník *Balenciaga stripes*
velvet and frame

137

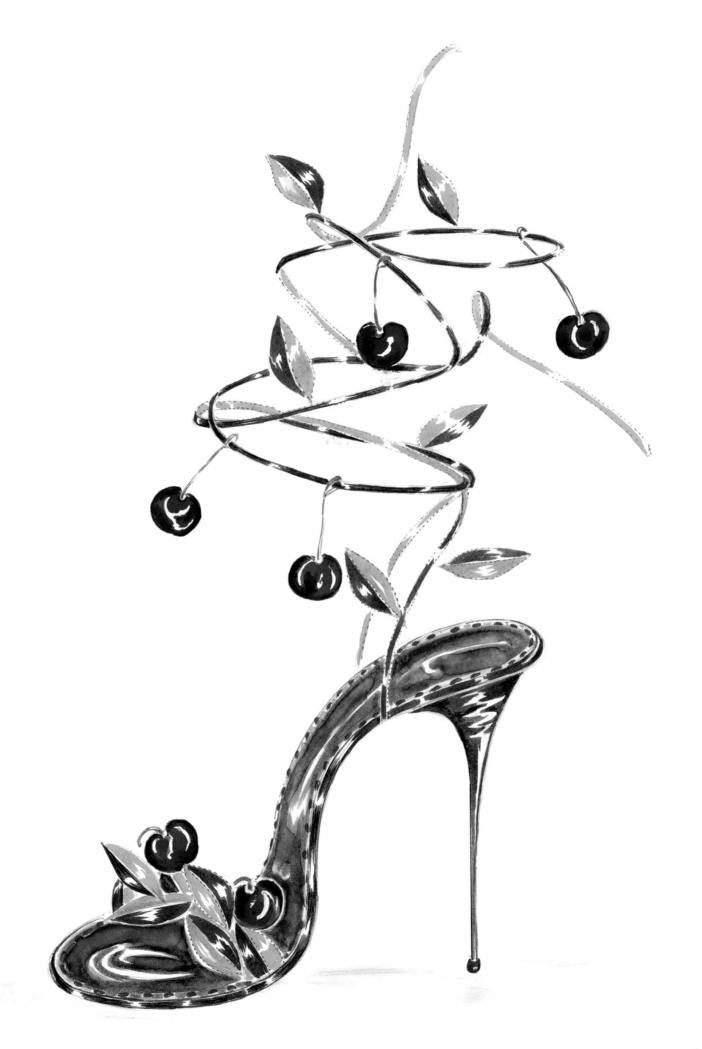

GAMOCHONIA · OCTOPUS ·

140

'Eccentric, exuberant and obsessed, Manolo Blahník may be the best thing to happen to women's legs since the stairclimber.' DODIE KAZANJIAN

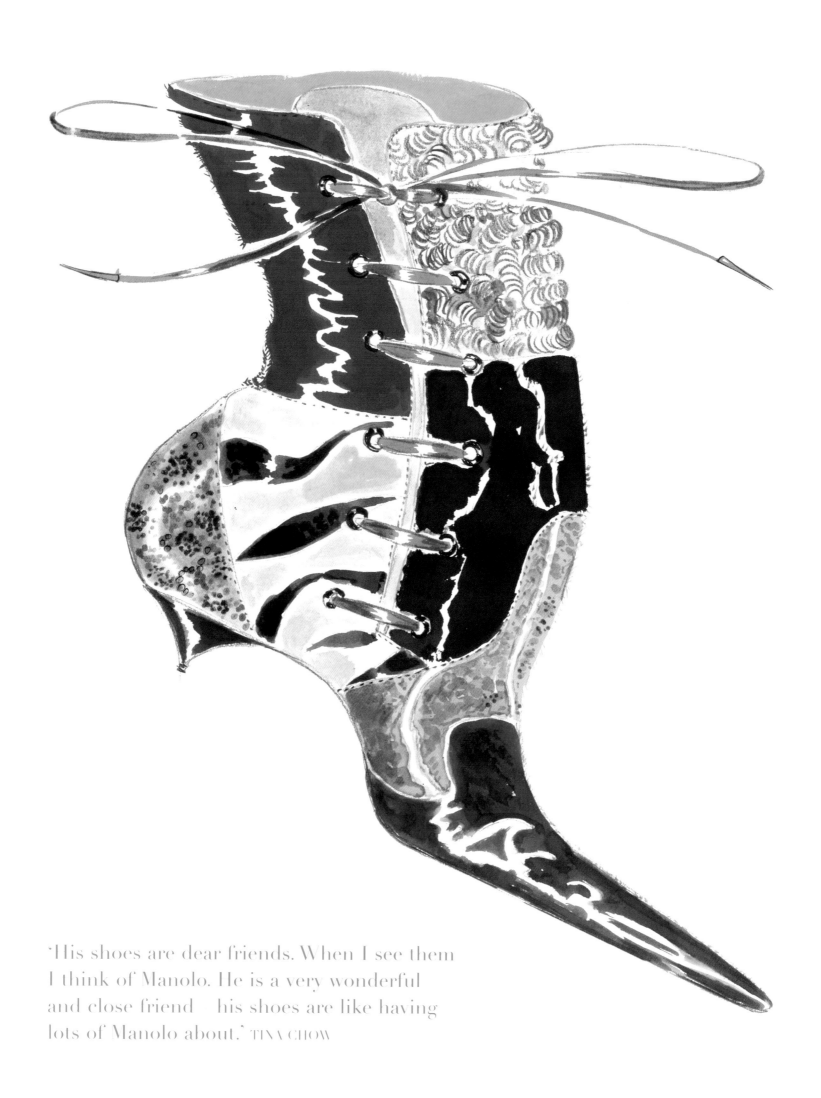

'His shoes are dear friends. When I see them
I think of Manolo. He is a very wonderful
and close friend — his shoes are like having
lots of Manolo about.' TINA CHOW

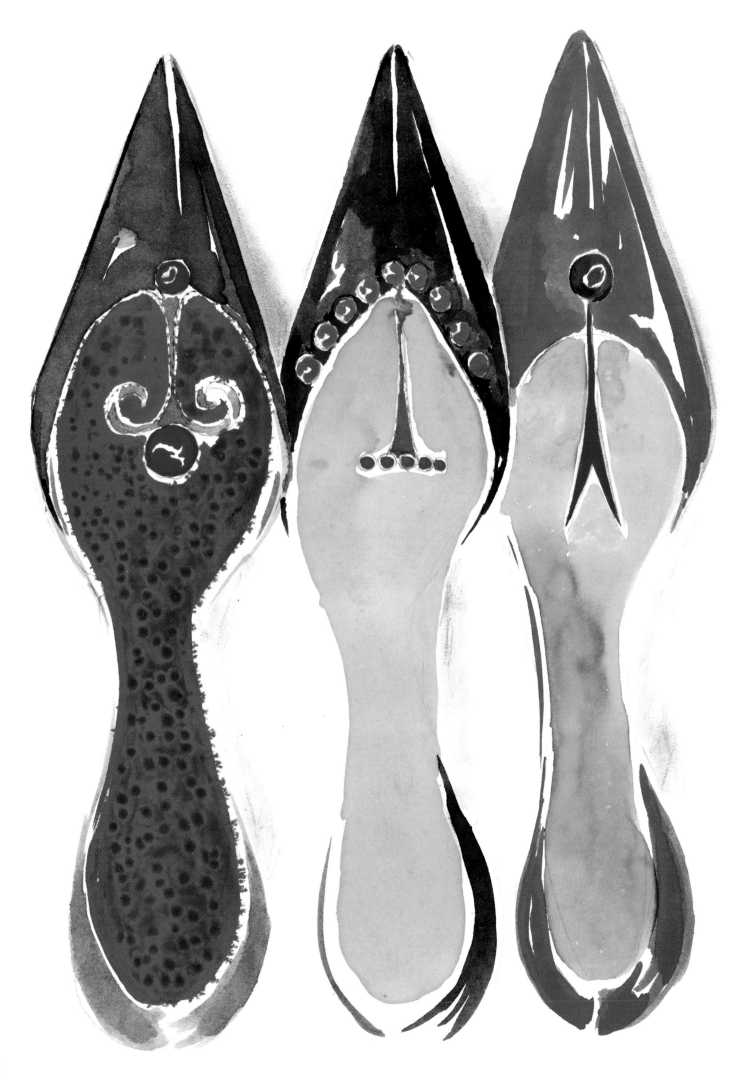

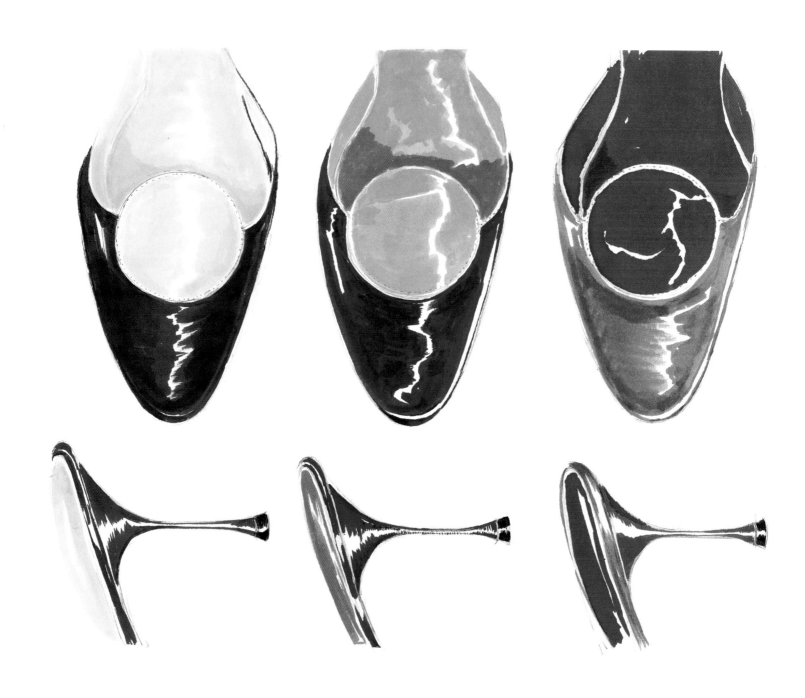

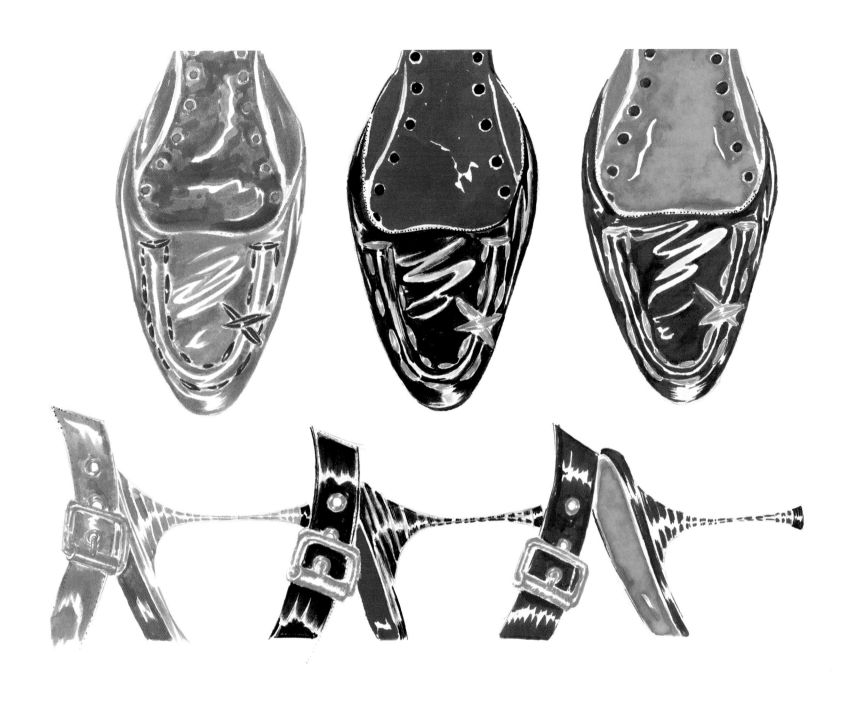

'For Blahník, it's not a question of searching for surface stimuli. When he begins to sketch his ideas for a new season they will be informed by the subconscious layer of sophisticated knowledge of art and architecture and his abiding love of the style of southern Europe.' COLIN McDOWELL

'Manolo once said to me: "My shoes are not fashion, they are gestures." I think of them as little parcels of pleasure offered to women. I think of him as a sorcerer of shoes, making them romantic, graceful, decorative, sensual. He can build more sexual arousal into a slither of suede or a slender heel than any other living shoemaker. Yet he is also a classicist in the great tradition of Andre Perugia or Roger Vivier in whose footsteps he follows to fashion immortality.'

SUZY MENKES

148

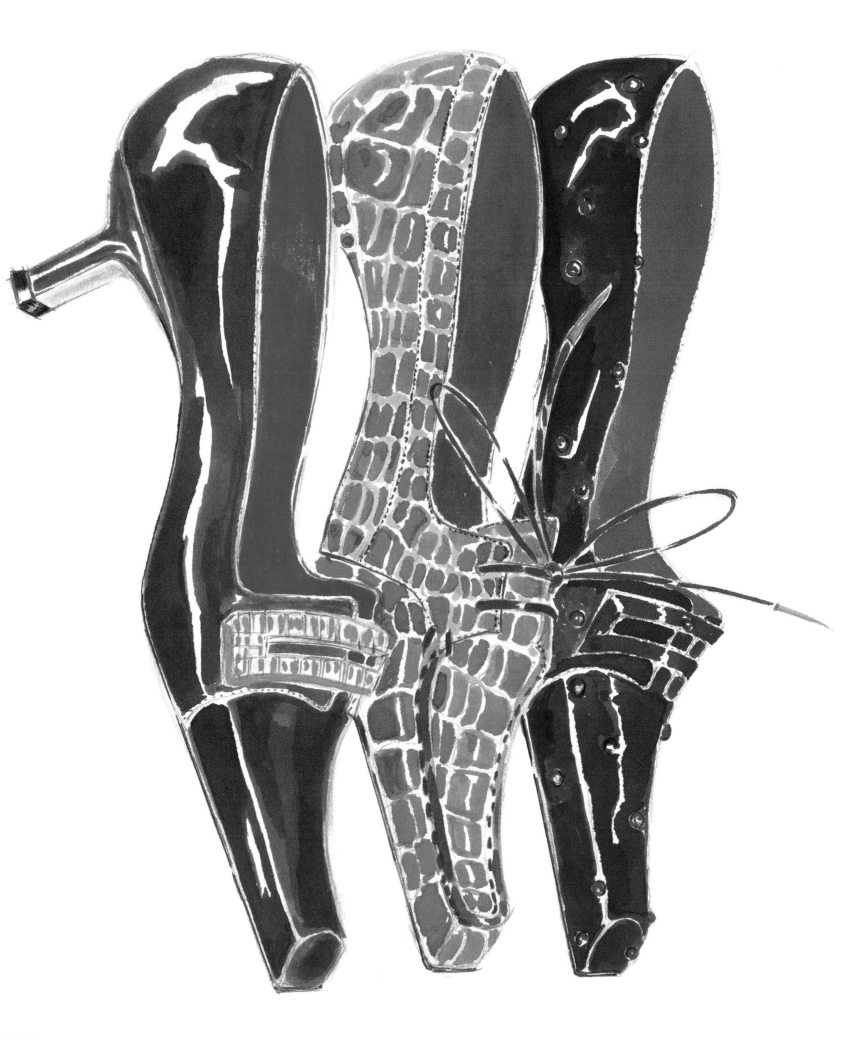

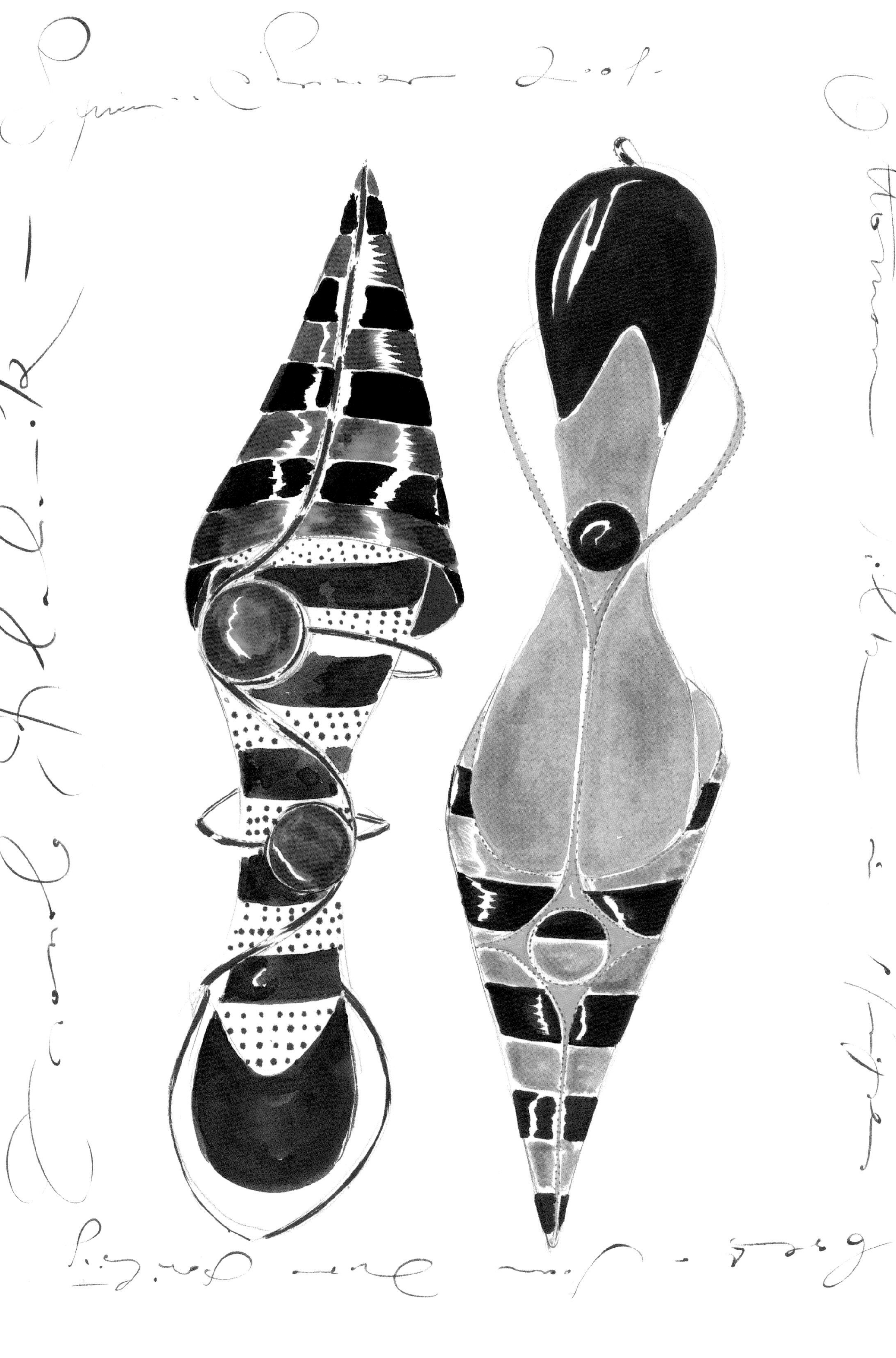
Spring Summer 2001
Manolo Blahnik

Empress Dowager Ci-Xi Beijing

Aluminium body – gèta Manolo Blahnik 2001

'Chaussée par Manolo, le pied d'une femme devient intelligent…' AZZEDINE ALAÏA

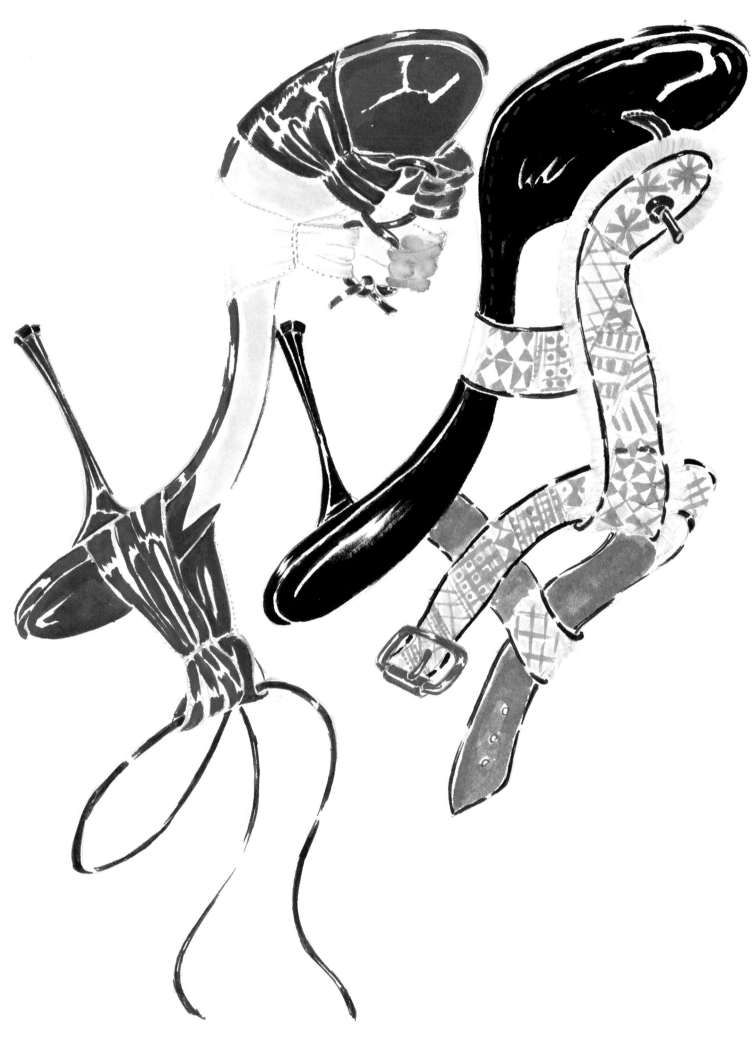

Style "Zamba"

Rifat Ozbek

'If God had wanted us to wear flat shoes, he wouldn't have invented Manolo Blahník.'
ALEXANDRA SHULMAN

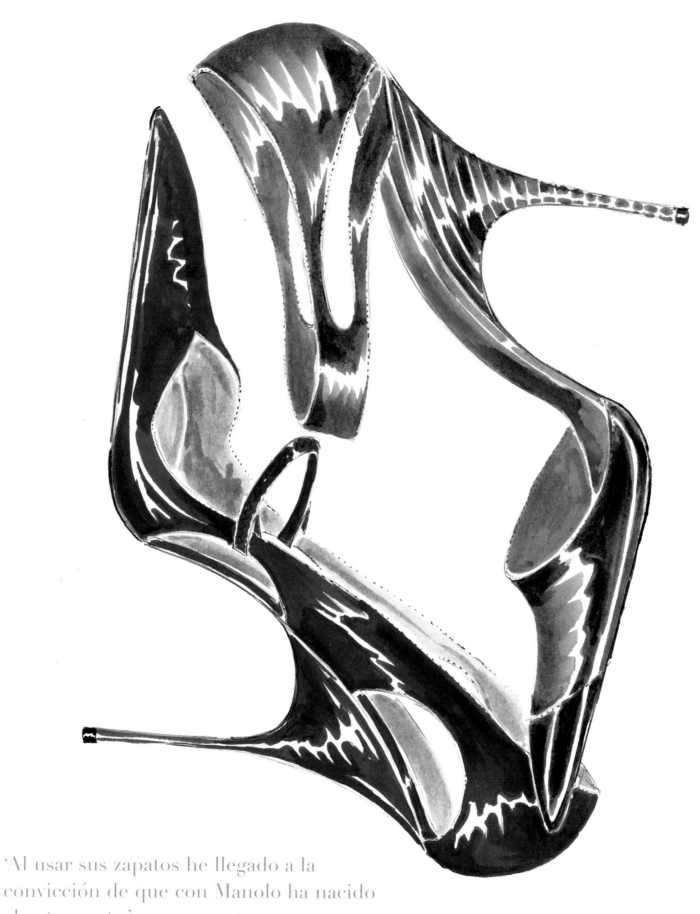

'Al usar sus zapatos he llegado a la
convicción de que con Manolo ha nacido
el octavo arte.' MARIBEL ARROCHA LUGO

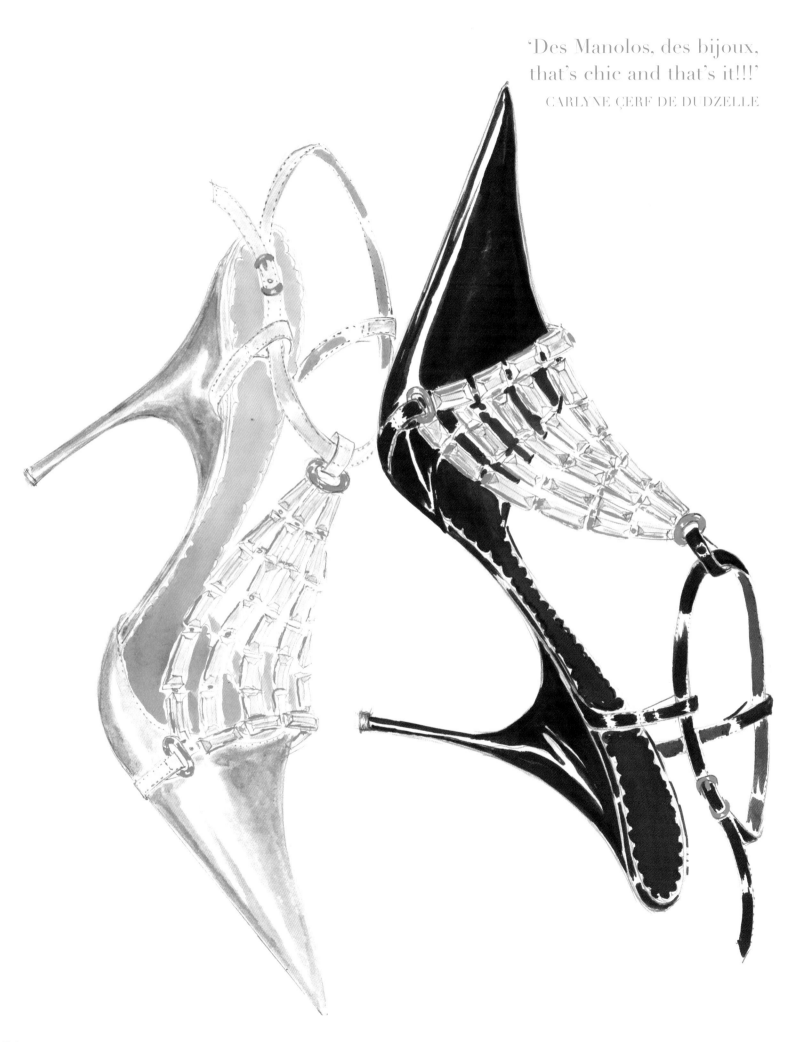

'Des Manolos, des bijoux, that's chic and that's it!!!'
CARLYNE CERF DE DUDZELLE

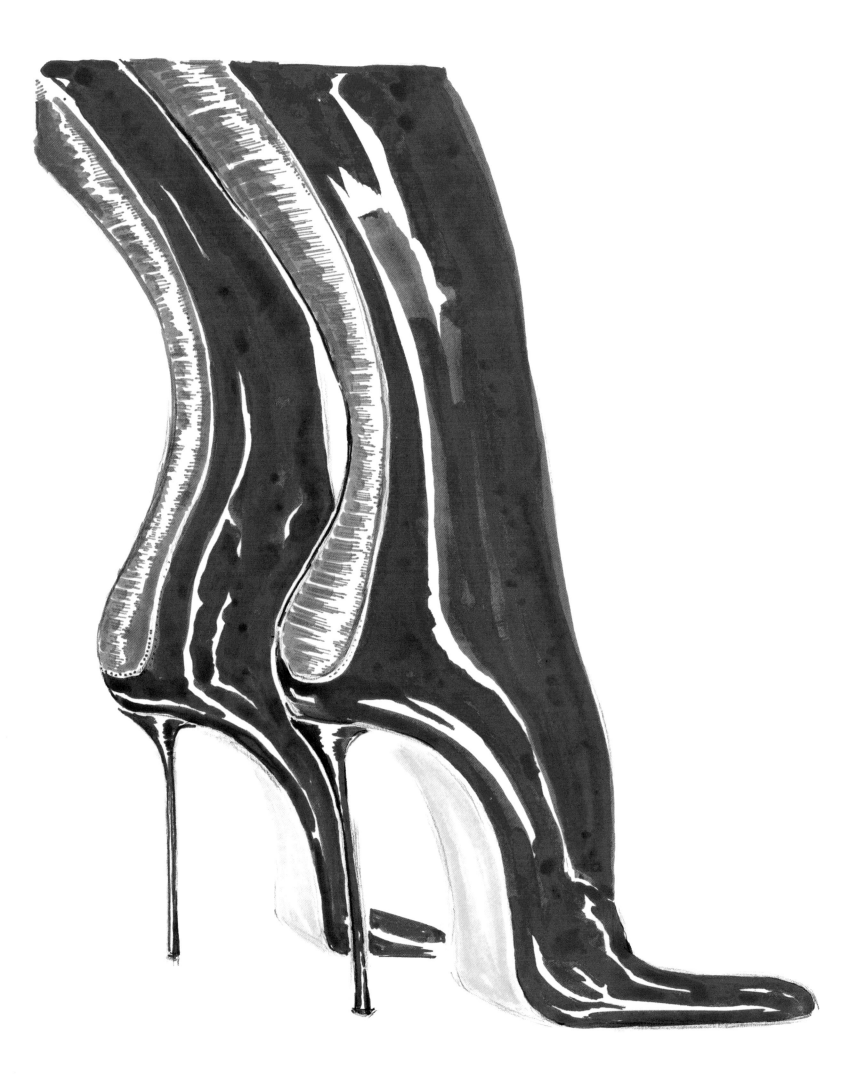

'Manolos – as in all you need are your Manolos and a dash of red lipstick – has crept into the vernacular and become not just the word that describes the world's most desirable shoes, but a kind of generic term for a shoe that is otherwise indescribably haute.' SHANE WATSON

'My Manolos are the first thing I see when I wake up, and the framed illustration Manolo drew for me is the last thing I see before I go to sleep.' CAMILLA MORTON

Manolo Blahnik — Spain

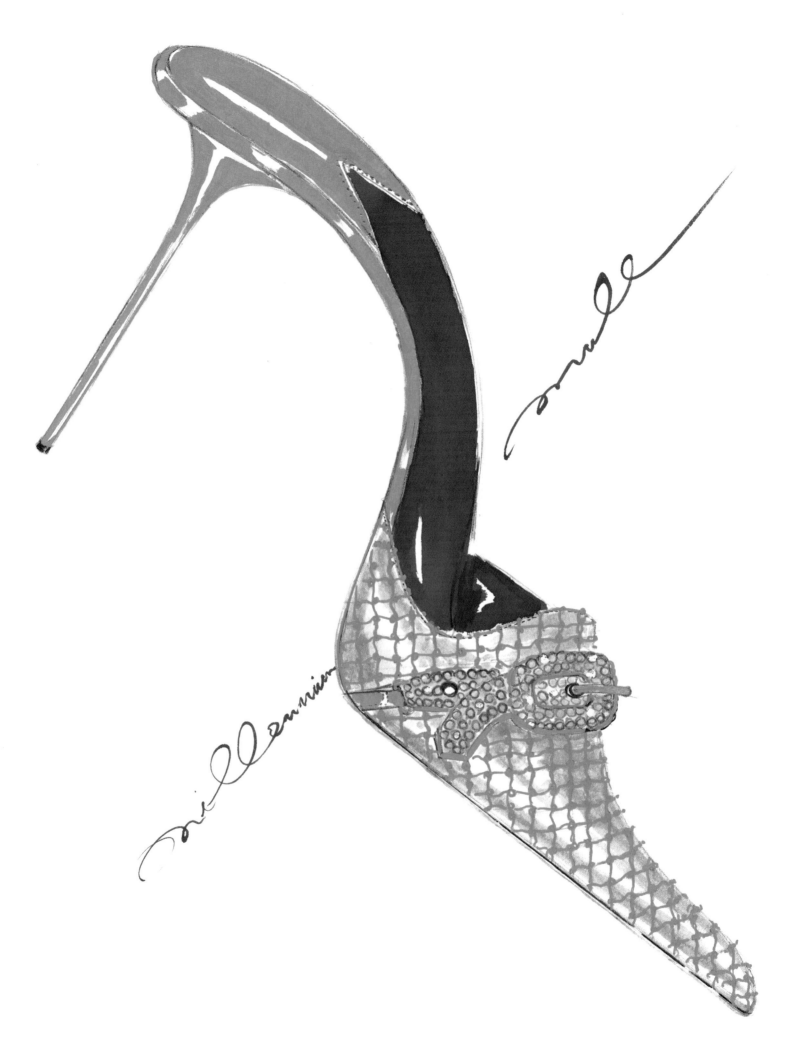

Manolo Blahnik 2000. Style: Cienza, with silver belts

'I guess the whole of my life is an adventure I lead in Manolo's shoes – and I can confirm to you that I am never without my Manolo shoes in my dreams.'
PALOMA PICASSO

'His shoes are slut pumps.
You just put on your Manolos
and you automatically find
yourself saying "Hi, sailor"
to every man that walks by.'
JOAN RIVERS

'1. Fabulous applause to the leg.
 2. The way a girl learns to walk.
 3. A look and feel you never forget!'
CANDY PRATTS-PRICE

'Owning a pair of Manolos is like
owning a gem.' NATI ABASCAL

'When I met Manolo, I quizzed him on tips for becoming an accessory designer. He said: "My dear, you must be better informed and more knowledgeable than a fashion designer because what you make can be worn with everything and anything. But when you design you must forget all that, and do exactly as you please." Wonderful, perceptive, irreverent, elegant and charming advice. Just like Manolo and his wonderful shoes.' STEPHEN JONES

Summer *Manolo Blahnik* 2003.

STYLE PERFIDIA

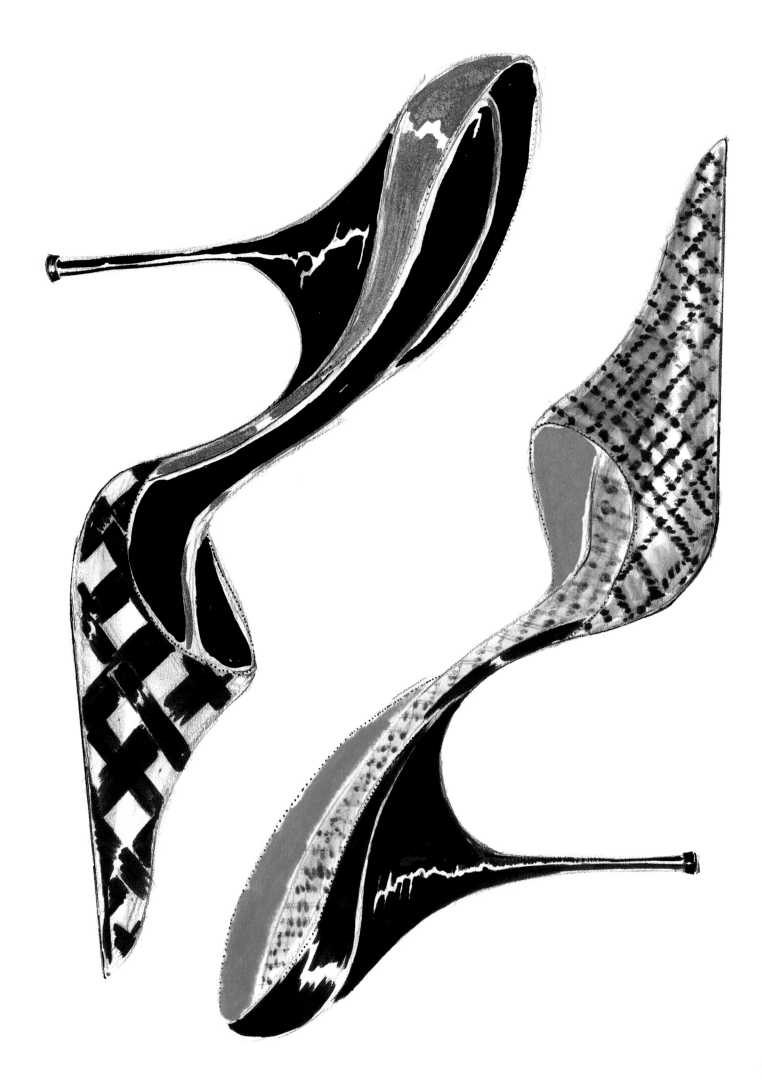

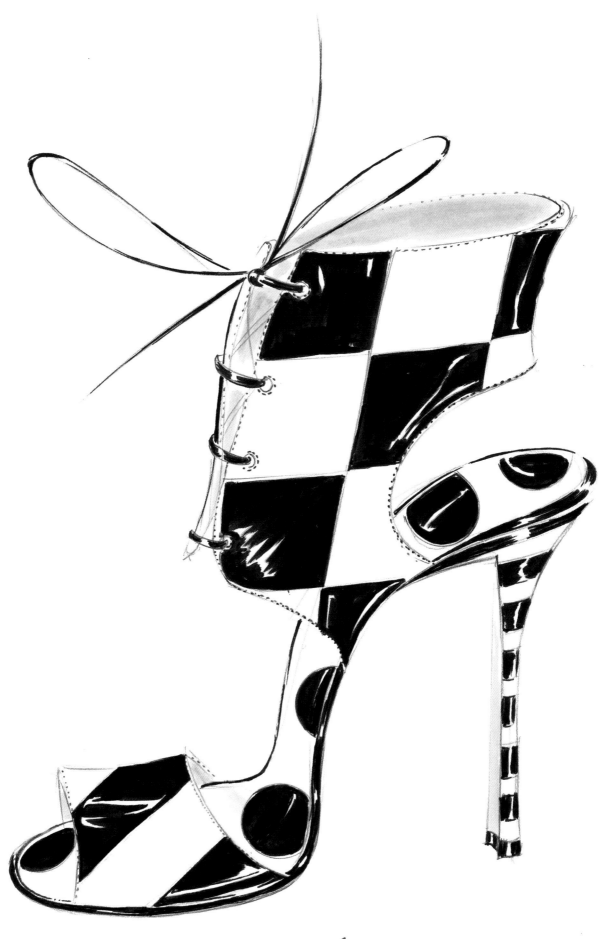

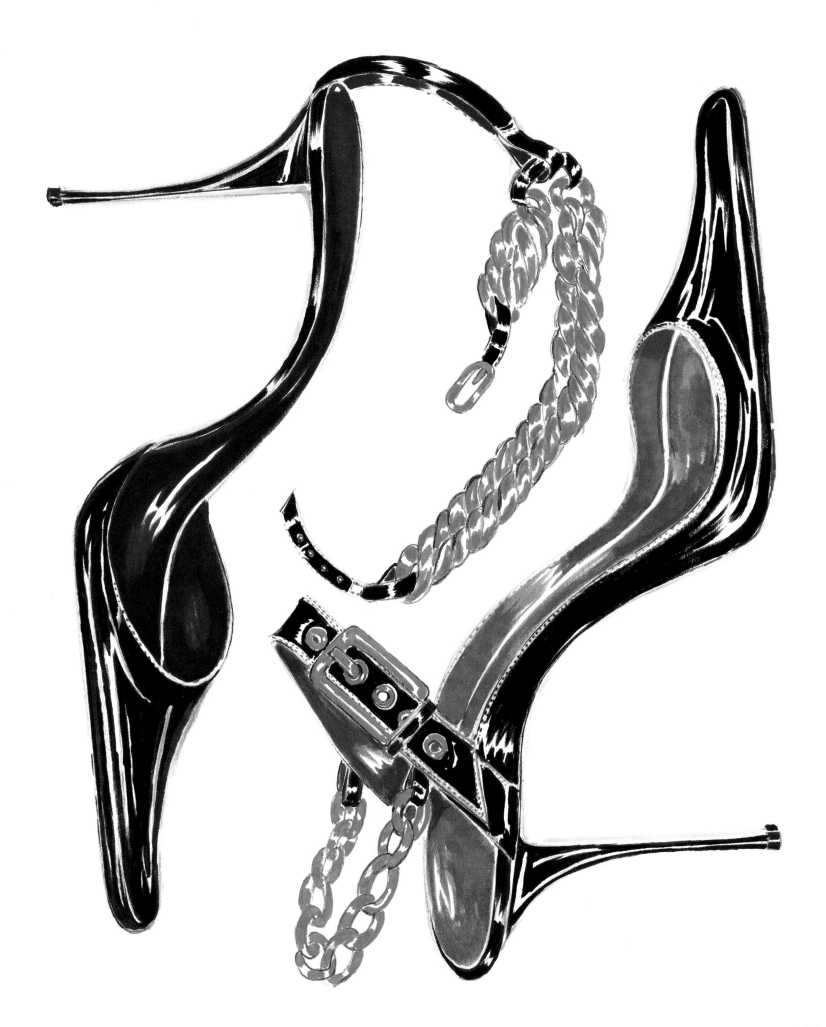

'They are strappy, sexy as hell.
The shoe itself is like a woman.'
SANDRA BERNHARD

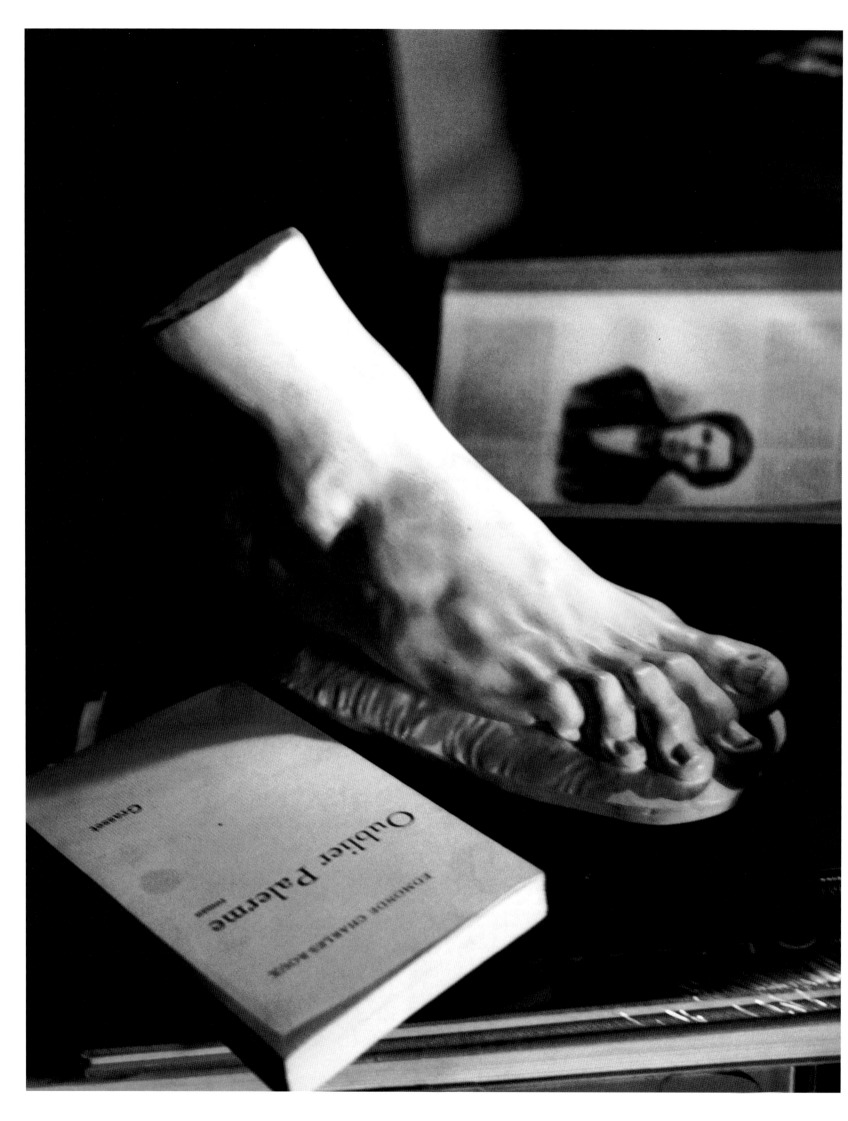

liking 'feets'

I knew Manolo before there were shoes in his life. Looking at his work, I can say that all that makes it what it is, was there, solidly all along. Manolo is the same man, now as then, absolutely, and this shows great personal integrity. At this point, of course, it's hard to imagine the man without the shoes – it's such a good fit. But it wasn't always so: Manolo could have gone in any number of directions. When, one day in the early 1970s, he said he was going to help some friends with the shoes they were hoping to sell in a tiny shop in Old Church Street, I wondered what he knew about shoemaking. He said something about liking 'feets', how they were the only part of the anatomy that he had any interest in – but the statement came imbedded in a tirade of generally absurd opinions, most enhanced for effect to the point where I would mentally turn down the volume and pathetically nod. Time has shown that the foot was more than the *passion du jour*. Unable to benefit from Manolo's shoes by wearing them, I am fascinated by how they are such a distillate of everything Manolo is – how true they are to him. He will give you the names of people and titles of books and movies, every inspiration that keeps him alive, and over a period of thirty-four years, he has never wavered. Manolo has always followed his own whim, often radically against the grain of fashion. During times when fashion has shown impatience with the arrival of the future, and embraced the new and weird seemingly for the sake of it, some have been exasperated by Manolo's refusal to join in. But women, seduced by how their legs and postures are transformed when they slip on a pair of Blahníks, don't care: in the end, what makes a woman look best proves irresistible, and therein lies one of the secrets to the success of Manolo Blahník. There are other ingredients, like dogged determination and relentless hard work. What has driven Manolo to the extent that his has become this awkward (thus memorable) household name? Greed? Certainly not. I ventured to speculate, long ago, that he might have been a spoilt brat (we were watching the child actor Freddie Bartholomew mama-ing and papa-ing his way through a Hollywood Dickens) and I wondered aloud if there was a similarity between FB and the boy Manolo, the only time I have seen his colour rise. He answered 'You know, it's true....' Rather, he has seen it as his own responsibility to maintain an auto-pampered state, manifested in his impeccable finery, the environments he has created for his pleasure, and his generosity to those he cares about. Hawk-eyed attention to detail and intolerance for compromise have benefited all he's done, yet cannot make for a simple life, and my guess is he finds living with himself a chore. Understand, this is someone who views the state of manicure as the number one human virtue. An outrageous brand of humility accompanies all this: Manolo constantly deprecates everything admirable about himself while telling you how ahead of your time and talented you are. And just plain outrageousness. All along I have marvelled at how his polite-ish madcap behaviour never essentially cut into his ascent. Bless the English for their taste for eccentricity, which gave this man a garden in which to bloom. He has returned the favour with his loyalty, which has kept him close to the places and people he loves. His true friends can attest. Personally, I can trace much of my current life to our chance meeting, proof that life is shaped by unpredictable events, and how important they can be. But the driving force behind Manolo's manic toil is the satisfaction of seeing the product finally realised as a true reflection of its inspiration. Art has seen a great many expressions in recent times. Here come the shoes!

ERIC BOMAN
Photographer

the step

'Your things are so witty,
part of the past, but so modern.'
CECIL BEATON

into possibility

To slip on desire and to fasten delicacy around your ankle – crocodile slipped through a ruby buckle like a feather of a key unlocking a jewel box – Manolo's shoes are about openings, about beginnings, about the leap into the hoped-for and the unnerving high of the certainty of feeling perfection. The curious, complex but splendid world of fashion is veined with feints and traps of illusion. It is fuelled by surface, play and insecurity. Disappointment festers at the back of the closet, lurking among those things we bought, uncertain of their real proportion, fit, line – in the obsessive heartbeat of our desire to consume the new. Manolo's shoes are forever new, reinventing everything we wear as they never disappoint. The miracle of his reinvention of the way we move is like Haute Couture – his work is about line and definition and grace. Colour, texture, angle, jewel, strap, eyelet and buckle…refined, brutal, sensuous, arch, joyous – this is the aesthetic unique to the elegance of Manolo Blahník. And all of this without beginning to understand the secret dynamics – the construction of the shoes – that complex surgery that lifts and angles the foot so that you walk like a dream of yourself. To wear a pair of Manolo's shoes is like dancing with the most fabulous dancer ever…it is the tango of your life. Only Manolo understands the camber of making aspiration a reality.

AMANDA, LADY HARLECH
Consultant

captions

22   Self-portrait as a mule, (2000).

25   The first shoe, sketched in 1971.

26   *Warsuma* (1971). Electric blue suede top, red suede ankle ties. 125mm rubber crepe heel. Used by Ossie Clarke.

28   Top: *Pilar* (1974). Black and white nappa kid Op-Art shoe. Striped back and ankle strap. Spotted front and 50mm heel. Bottom: *Piaggi* (1974). Black and white striped nappa kid lace-up bottine, with open back and front. 50mm heel.

30   *Brick* (1971). Cork sole, covered in black patent leather, green patent leather upper. Prototype

developed and made by Manolo Blahník. Used by Kansai Yamamoto.

32   *Warholia* (1978). Oriental court shoe in chrome yellow suede, violet kid lining. 105mm heel. Drawing in the manner of Andy Warhol.

33   *Oum* (1978). Oriental court shoe in shocking pink suede, pink kid lining. 105mm heel. Drawing in the manner of Andy Warhol.

34   *Scarlett* (1979). Walking shoe, in the style of a golf shoe, in brown suede, with red suede 105mm heel. Green, red and violet fringe. Green kid lining.

36   *Laza* (1975). Lettuce green nappa leather sandal,

with acid green lining. 125mm rounded heel.

38 *Iey* (1971). Two-tone brilliant green sandal with suede straps, leather ties and uppers. Berries in red kid. 105mm heel. Remade as *Ossie* in 1997.

39 *Pimienta* (1977). Décolleté sandal in black kid with red plastic cones. Straps in fine nappa leather. 105mm heel.

40 *Titi* (1979). Sandal in panther print pony (natural cowhide) lined in red kid. Sock in leopard print pony. 105mm heel in red kid.

41 *Paloma* (1972). Pump in leopard print pony, with yellow lining and black patent ankle strap. 105mm heel in printed pony.

42 *Catwoman* (1974). Black suede bottine, with silk/cotton mix fake fur trim. Leather laces. 50mm heel.

43 *Knott* (1975). Red fine nappa kid mule, with double knot detail. Sock lined in red and cream patchwork leather. 105mm heel. Remade in 1985 as *Camerana*.

44 Top: *Moronia* (1972). Gold nappa kid sandal, lined in pink. 105mm heel. Bottom: *Helvin* (1977). Gold nappa leather sandal, lined in pink. 105mm Penta heel. Red patent version in V & A archives.

45 *Muir* (1976). Antiqued gold nappa leather and navy suede shoe, with gold stitching. Gold Carreté 90mm heel. Used by Jean Muir.

46 *BJ* (1978). Named after Bianca Jagger. Mocha kid leather sandal, fastened with metal rings. 125mm heel.

48 *Babilonia* (1972). Black and white leopard pony shoe, with zebra print pony heel. Black leather trellis ankle tie. 105mm heel.

49 *Intolerance* (1972). Blue leopard print pony, with ankle strap. 105mm heel.

50 *Gruyère* (1979). Violet kid with orange nappa circles and strap. Aluminium base. No heel.

51 *Jubilee* (1976). Shoe in red and blue suede, with red leather tie. 100mm twisted metal heel.

54 *Regalis* (1980). Shoe in black, white, red and blue kid. 105cm striped, round heel.

56 *Sevilla* (1980). Black suede mule, lined in red, with red suede spherical decorations. 50mm heel.

57 Preliminary drawings for Top: *Bag* (1980) satin court shoe. Bottom: *Orienta* 1980, satin mule.

58 *Satina* (1985). Lace-up bootie in lozenge embroidered satin. 90mm heel.

59 *Linda* (1985). Ottoman silk court shoe, with leather ankle strap, and pleated point d'esprit bib. Orange lining. 105mm heel.

60 *Window Gropius* (1998). Boot made of strips of black patent leather.

62 *Iman* (1982). High-tongued flat shoe in tiger printed pony.

63 *Orientalia* (1986). Mule in antiqued gold leaf lizard skin, with decorative panel of baroque pearls, semi-precious stones and beads. Used by Bill Blass and Carolina Herrera.

64 *Perry* (1981). Rust sable trimmed kid bootie with horn toggles. Used by Perry Ellis.

65 *Directoire* (1985). Flat boot made of velvet strips,

with painted astrakhan collar.

66 *Laurelia* (1988). Green satin d'Orsay shoe, with suede leaves, and wooden berries. 90mm heel.

67 *Caduta* (1988). Mule in pale blue chiffon with silver threads, edged in blue, green and red. 90mm heel.

69 *Avion* (1982). One piece aluminium base with transparent plastic straps. 105mm heel.

70 *Ring* (1984). Red suede sandal with antiqued metal rings and low platform sole. 105mm heel.

71 *La Madonna* (1988). Mule in violet and red suede, with top strap going round the heel. Bronze halo on front and star-shaped studs. 105mm heel.

72 *Rodriga* (1988). Flat, crepe soled lace-up boots in satin and velvet. Used by Isaac Mizrahi.

74 *Liz* (1986). Violet silk satin d'Orsay shoe, lined in pink satin. 105mm heel.

75 *Cecilia* (1987). Evening court shoe in pink silk satin, bordered with silk flowers. 70mm heel.

76 Top: *Argolida* (1985). Flat shoe in zebra printed satin, lined in yellow silk, with gold leather straps. Centre: *Migdalia* (1985). Flat shoe in navy and grey ottoman silk, lined in spotted silk, with navy leatherstraps. Bottom: *Algeria* (1985). Flat open-toed shoe in black and white kid.

77 Top: *Diana* (1984). Flat shoe in midnight blue velvet with gold silk net. Bottom: *Imperia* (1984). Mule in violet silk velvet, with cabochon pearls, heel lined with pavé strass.

79 *Martha* (1986). Pump in red silk taffeta, with silk faille ribbon straps. 50mm heel. Used by Rifat Ozbek.

83 *Arcadia* (1998). Boot in royal blue satin, with baby blue satin back and 105mm heel. Yellow Mokuba laces. Used by Antonio Berardi.

84 *Poiret* (1998) Mule in dark brown silk satin with chinchilla tongue, lined in vivid blue satin. 105mm heel. Also in real silver mesh.

85 *Page* (1998) 'Hoffman cage' shoe in midnight blue satin, with 'cage' in midnight blue suede. 105mm heel.

86 *Perdicca* (1998). Flat pump in ottoman silk, with border in contrasting grosgrain braid. Also in pony.

88 *Jenne* (1996). Clear plastic mule, with red satin ribbon ties. 105mm metal 'Brancusi' heel. Used by John Galliano. Worn by Kate Moss.

89 *Herva* (1996). Knee-high zig-zag lace-up boot, in black patent leather. 105mm heel.

90 *Apollonia* (1990). Ruby red silk satin shoe, lined in violet and yellow spotted pony. 105mm heel.

91 *Shanghai* (1995). Chrome yellow silk shantung mule, lined in Chinese red satin. 105mm heel.

92 *Brazil* (1997). Sandal in blood red nappa kid, with Velcro fastenings. 105mm heel.

93 *Claudia* (1997). Acid green mule in fine grain kid, lined in dark green kid. 105mm heel.

95 *Guge* (1997). Architectural sandal inspired by the New York Guggenheim museum, in navy and mustard leather. 105mm heel.

96 *Shinyuku* (1998). Shoe in burnt brown cervo, with

dark blue silk nylon trimmings. Velcro fastenings and turquoise lining. 105mm heel.

97 *Nikkai* (1998). Yellow nappa kid shoe with black mesh inserts and Velcro fastenings. 105mm heel.

98 *Rideau* (1997). Amber satin shoe, with buckled velvet Mokuba ribbons and silk fringe. 105mm heel.

99 *Fiore* (1998). Gold ottoman silk mule, with roses in red nappa. 105mm heel. Used by John Galliano for Givenchy Haute Couture.

100 *Phoenix* (1997). Sandal adorned with 'palm leaves' in three shades of green kid on a 105mm plastic wedge covered in ochre kid. Project for John Galliano.

101 *Tullio* (1999). Open backed buckled shoe in forest green suede, lined in ruby red kid, with glove stitching in tomato red. 105mm heel.

102 *Tiber* (1998). Roman sandal in red kid, decorated with antiqued bronze and amber cabochons. 105mm heel.

103 *Caligu* (1992). Shoe in tobacco brown silk moiré, embroidered with tufts of violet silk thread and decorated with rough horn. 105mm heel and lining in magenta nappa.

104 *Samio* (1992). Mule in chartreuse green ottoman silk, decorated with 'strawberries' made of crochet and beads. 105mm heel.

105 *Acero* (1990). Berry red suede mule, with 'bamboo twig' 105mm heel and straps in three tones of green suede and kid. Lined in yellow kid.

106 *Natale* (1994). Dark green silk velvet boot, with bird head and feather trim. 105mm heel.

107 *Senso* (1998). Back-lacing boot in a patchwork of various printed ottoman silks by Taroni, Lisio and Ratti, with gold bead fringing. 105mm heel.

108 Top: *Peineta* (renamed *Geina*) (1999). Summer mule in blue linen with straps in black nappa. 90mm heel. Bottom: *Joyu* (1999). Mule in natural lizard, with magenta leather ties decorated with African beads. 50mm heel in magenta leather.

110 *Watusi* (1997). Back-lacing boot in leopard printed pony decorated with raffia trim, wooden buttons, beading and tassles. 105mm bead decorated heel.

112 *Masai* (1997). Sandal in black suede, decorated with black, red, yellow and turquoise beads and mother-of-pearl buttons. 110mm heel. Created for John Galliano at Christian Dior Haute Couture.

113 *Orsona* (1997). Open back and front boot in giraffe print linen, with back zip fastening. Lined in leopard print linen, and decorated with painted wooden beads. 115mm heel. Created for John Galliano at Christian Dior Haute Couture.

114 Left: *Tonta* (1997). Mule in burnt orange linen, with white kid scalloped trim. 90mm heel. Centre: *Oberdan* (1977). Grey cultured pearl thong, with ankle ties in green kid. Right: *Lengua* (1977). Fuchsia silk mule, with glass 'berries'. 90mm heel.

115 *Thebu* (1997). Thong sandal in black Arriana silk with red coral decorations. 50mm heel.

116 *Benabu* (1999) Summer sandal in nappa with contrasting 50mm heel. Thong in clear plastic.

117 *Armadillo* (1999). Mule in Fuchsia, violet and orange nappa on heel-less aluminium body.

118 *Gheria* (1998). Mule in antiqued gold nappa leather, with clear plastic strap. 105mm heel in cast brass.

119 *Tella* (1997). Two-tone shoe in fuchsia nappa leather and ochre kid on 100mm Clavo 'screw' heel in fuchsia.

120 *Galli* (1995). Red Ottoman silk shoe, with straps in champagne nappa, on a gold-leafed wedge heel. Created for John Galliano.

121 *Hebilla* (1996). Mule in striped satin by Canepa. Plain satin buckle support between toes, and side fastening buckles. 105mm heel.

122 *Manby* (1997). 'African' sandal decorated with ebony, shell and bone beads. Lined in leopard printed linen. 90mm heel in red kid. Used by John Galliano.

124 *Mopium* (1998). Flat shoe in Ottoman silk, with marabou feather trim, and kid ties.

125 *Popea* (1998). Giraffe printed pony, lined in royal blue nappa, with long haired Tibetan goat collar, and ties in gold nappa leather. Metal tipped 50mm heel.

126 *Lanelo* (1999). Natural cowskin boot, lined in fuchsia. 105mm heel. Used by John Galliano.

131 *Untitled* (2000). Yellow Chantilly silk with red 'blood' detail made in Viennese crystal and metal scissors. Unfinished project for Anna Piaggi. Italian *Vogue*.

132 *Venusa* (2002). Brunswick zebra print linen sandal with brown leather bow, and natural lining. 90mm heel. Created for Nicole Kidman.

133 *Tricidia* (2002). Black Bretagne kid sandal with chrome buckles, lined in punched red-brown leather. 105mm heel.

134 *Cadiz* (2001). Yellow satin heel-less mule, decorated with yellow and red tassles, lined in green satin. Similar version with closed, pointed toe and heel.

136 Left: *Leiga* (2002). T-bar shoe in red satin with red Venetian glass beads. 105mm heel. Right: *Giotto* (2002). Leaf green satin shoe, with ankle strap decorated with glass Ventian beads. 105mm heel.

137 *Quadro* (2000). 'Picture frame' shoe in striped velvet with nappa trim. 105mm metal heel.

138 *Cereza* (2003). Sandal in two tones of green suede, with ties in kid, lacquered 'cherries' and brown kid lining. 105mm metal heel.

139 *Trillo* (2003). Shoe in green linen, with embroidered front, decorated with Culantrillo leaves in kid, with metal wire support. Lined in dark green kid. 105mm heel.

140 *Gamochonia* (2000). Shoe in beige suede, with embroidered octopus and tentacles climbing up the leg. 105mm heel.

142 *Lulamae* (1999). Side-lacing bottine in a patchwork of printed pony, astrakhan, and Tibetan goat. 30mm heel.

143 *Volterra* (2001). 50mm heeled mule with different embroideries and decolette details.

144 *Nagoya* 2002 . Linen mule with nappa disc detail and lining. 90mm titanium heel.

145 *Gallo* 2002 . Sandal in waxed Bretagne kid, with hand stitched 'mocassin' front, chrome buckle on ankle strap. 105mm titanium heel.

147 Top: *Lono* 2000 and Bottom: *Atlantico* 2000 . Slingbacks in Bretagne kid, with horn tablets as medallions. 90mm Picabia heel.

148 *Pascalare* 2000 . Knee-length boot in fuchsia crocodile printed pony, on a stacked 105mm heel.

149 Left: *Info* 2000 . Black satin evening shoe with rectangular German crystal buckle. 50mm heel. Centre: *Falcione* 2000 . Shoe in supple Louisiana crocodile, on 50mm heel. Right: *Info* 2000 . Version in purple ostrich with leather appliqué replacing buckle. 50mm heel.

150 Left: *Vunda* 2001 . Right: *Truca* 2001 . Shoes in striped Ottoman silk, with leather ties and spherical decorations. 70mm heel.

151 Top: *Cersea* 2001 . Mule in baby blue and white striped linen, with baby blue kid tongue and ties. Yellow kid lining. 70mm heel. Bottom: *Selenice* 2001 . Yellow and black leather mule with red lining. 70mm heel.

152 *Ci-Xi* 2001 . Oriental shoe in yellow Chinese silk crepe, with lettuce green Ottoman silk lining, and shocking pink nappa trimmings. Black lacquer. 105mm heel.

153 *Jetta* 2001 . Japanese inspired jetta in zebra line with violet silk and leopard with ties in violet silk. Four-heeled base in aluminium.

154 Left: *Zibar* 2003 . Afrocuban sandal in hyena printed pony, with imitation bone strips, lined in blood red kid. 70mm heel. Right: *Trombo* 2003 . Sandal in chocolate brown lizard, with irregular shaped bone accessories. 105mm heel.

155 Left: *Prasia* 2003 . Sandal in multicoloured pore velours with ribbon ties. 105mm heel. Right: *Ermesina* 2003 . Guadeloupe print pony sandal with green wool and black kid trim, black kid lining and trim. 90mm heel.

156 *Zamba* 2000 . Open foot and back boot in plantation rubber, with toe-ring and lining in turquoise nappa. 90mm bamboo heel. Used by Rifat Ozbek.

157 *Cuba* 2003 . Shoe in pleated and hand stitched nappa, lined in teal nappa, with t-bar strap decorated with imitation bone rings. 90mm heel in wood veneer, lined in teal nappa.

159 *Ortensia* 2003 . Sandal in ruby red linen, with chrome ring detail, ties in ruby red lustrous nappa, lining in chartreuse nappa. 90mm heel. After Oscar Niemeyer.

160 Left: *Sulfu* 2001 . Rusty red wool flannel court shoe, with cut-out side panels, lined in violet kid. 105mm 'stacked' heel. Right: *Benga* 2001 . Moss green shoe in nappa and suede with 105mm 'stacked' heel.

161 *Lolo* 2001 . Satin evening shoe in poppy red or lilac, with rectangular-shaped diamante decoration forming a triangle reminiscent of a Christmas tree.

162 *Clotoback* 2000 . Pink knee high boots, in shiny leather, with elasticated panel up the back. 105mm heel.

164 Top: *Concul* 2001 . Slingback in tomato red and black crepe de chine with diamante buckle, lined in fuchsia with half metal 90mm heel. Bottom: *Cacatoes* 2001 . Slingback in silver thread brocade with floral weave, and old-fashioned marquisite buckle suspended above the foot with turquoise leather ties. 105mm half metal heel.

166 *Dilé* 2001 . Botanical shoe, with tresses of leather, garlanded with leather and red beads. Homage to Pablo and Delia with Grace Coddington of American Vogue.

167 *Lyonnia* 2001 . Pink leather sandal, with buds of Lyonnaise Caligulata ties. 105mm heel.

168 *Cleota* 2000 . Champagne nappa shoe with toe in silver grey satin, covered with a delicate silver mesh, and a diamanté strass belt and fuchsia lining.

169 *Cienza* 2000 . Strappy sandals, embellished with Turkish silver bells and turquoise stones. Lined in different colours of kid. 105mm heel.

171 *Atala* 2000 . Squared toed slingback in red wool flannel embroidered with Empress Elizabeth gilet motif. Lined in black kid. 105mm heel.

172 *Kayapo* 2001 . Sandal in strips of red waxy kid decorated with old gold rivets. 105mm half metal heel.

173 *Finco* 2000 . Matt black leather mule, with a laced up front. 115mm heel.

174 *Franca* 2000 . Black kid mule, with white pony panel, lined in fuchsia kid. 105mm heel.

175 *Eames* 2001 . Sandal in rust and black patent leather. 105mm heel.

176 *Tortura* 2000 . Mule in oxblood silk chiffon, with wild coral decoration. Small coral decorations on ankle strap. 105mm heel.

177 Top: *Benevente* 2001 . Orange suede shoe with red stitching, leather heel and ties. Wild coral decorations. 105mm heel. Bottom: *Ponteros* 2001 . Mule in yellow crepe de chine, with coral rings and red satin heel.

179 *Perfidia* 2003 . Sandal inspired by Irving Penn's 1950s photograph of Don Cristobal Balenciaga's Balloon dress, in pleated brick red soft nappa. 105mm heel.

180 *Verdurin* 2001 . Mules in satin, plain and checkered silk velvets by Canepa, and plain nappa.

181 *Fangio* 2003 . Cutout boot in black and white leather, chequered flag motif, with spotted lining and striped 105mm heel.

182 Left: *Puri* 2002 . Black kid shoe, with heavy metal ankle strap. 105mm heel. Right: *Shaba* 2002 . Black kid mule with metal buckle and chain. 105mm heel.

this portfolio is for my mother

In a photograph taken by his
father, an 18-month-old
Manolo holds up his own shoe
to the camera.

special thanks

Manolo Blahník would like to thank everyone, friends and colleagues who have contributed with quotes and thoughts, without which this work would not have been possible. Special gratitude goes to Ms Anna Wintour for her generosity and support; to Michael Roberts for his photographs and his advice and to André Leon Talley, for his loyalty and encouragement. Thanks also to Ms Teresa Roviras, for her talent and understanding; to his sister Evangelina Blahník and her daughter Kristina, to Jamie Prieto, Ms Leslie Whittaker, Joe Fountain, Thomas Neurath, Neil Palfreyman, Clive Wilson and Gerhard Steidl for their invaluable help in putting this book together.

sources of quotations

24 'Shoe's Who: Manolo Blahník' by Joan Juliet Buck.
First published in British *Vogue*, December 1979.
© Condé Nast Publications. Reprinted by permission
of Condé Nast Publications.

29 'Fashion's Footman' by Amy Fine Collins.
First published in *Vanity Fair*, May 1995.
© Amy Fine Collins.

45 'Footnotes from Manolo Blahník' by Sarajane
Hoare. First published in British *Vogue*, September
1990. © Condé Nast Publications. Reprinted by
permission of Condé Nast Publications.

61 'History in the Taking' by Stephanie Theobald.
First published in *Harpers & Queen*, December
2001. © 2001 The National Magazine Company
Limited. Reprinted by permission of The National
Magazine Company Limited.

73 'Fashion's Footman' by Amy Fine Collins.
First published in *Vanity Fair*, May 1995.
© Amy Fine Collins.

75 'Fashion's Footman' by Amy Fine Collins.
First published in *Vanity Fair*, May 1995.
© Amy Fine Collins.

81 'High Heel Heaven' by Michael Specter.
First published in *The New Yorker*, 20 March, 2000.
© 2000 Michael Specter. Reprinted by permission
of International Creative Management, Inc.

84 'Fashion's Footman' by Amy Fine Collins.
First published in *Vanity Fair*, May 1995.
© Amy Fine Collins.

96 'Footnotes from Manolo Blahník' by Sarajane
Hoare. First published in British *Vogue*, September
1990. © Condé Nast Publications. Reprinted by
permission of Condé Nast Publications.

123 'Feets of Brilliance' by Dodie Kazanjian.
First published in American *Vogue*, March 1992.
© Dodie Kazanjian.

128 'High Heel Heaven' by Michael Specter.
First appeared in *The New Yorker*, 20 March, 2000.
© 2000 Michael Specter. Reprinted by permission
of International Creative Management, Inc.

133 'Piece of Kate'. First published in *Harpers & Queen*,

June 2002. © 2002 The National Magazine
Company Limited.

141 'Feets of Brilliance' by Dodie Kazanjian.
First published in American *Vogue*, March 1992.
© Dodie Kazanjian.

142 'Footnotes from Manolo Blahník' by Sarajane
Hoare. First published in British *Vogue*, September
1990. © Condé Nast Publications. Reprinted by
permission of Condé Nast Publications.

145 'Manolo Blahník' by Colin McDowell.
First published by Cassell & Co, 2000.
© 2000 Colin McDowell. Reprinted by permission
of Colin McDowell.

153 'Fashion's Footman' by Amy Fine Collins.
First published in *Vanity Fair*, May 1995.
© Amy Fine Collins.

158 'A Shoe With a View' by Alexandra Shulman. First
published in British *Vogue*, July 1994. © Condé
Nast Publications. Reprinted by permission of
Condé Nast Publications.

163 'High on Heels' by Shane Watson. First published
in British *Elle*, February 1995. © Hachette Emap
Magazines Ltd. Reprinted by permission of
Hachette Emap Magazines Ltd.

170 'High Heels and Desire' by Lucy Ferry.
First published in the *Independent on Sunday*,
24 July, 1994. © *Independent on Sunday*.
Reprinted by permission of *Independent on Sunday*.

172 'High Heel Heaven' by Michael Specter.
First appeared in *The New Yorker*, 20 March, 2000.
© 2000 Michael Specter. Reprinted by permission
of International Creative Management, Inc.

176 'Cumbre de la Elegancia' by Nati Abascal. First
appeared in Spanish *Vogue*, May 2002. © Condé
Nast Publications. Reprinted by permission of
Condé Nast Publications.

183 'High Heels and Desire' by Lucy Ferry.
First published in the *Independent on Sunday*, 24
July 1994. © *Independent on Sunday*. Reprinted by
permission of *Independent on Sunday*.

First published in the United Kingdom in 2003 by Thames & Hudson Ltd, 181A High Holborn, London WC1V 7QX

www.thamesandhudson.com

Reprinted 2003

Book designed by Teresa Roviras

British Library Cataloguing-in-Publication Data
A catalogue record for this book is available from the British Library

ISBN 0-500-28413-X

Printed and bound in Germany by Steidl Verlag und Druck